BEING ~~HAPPY~~ LUCKY

Recommendations

"*Happiness is Depressing* starts light-heartedly and takes you step by step to the causes of depression, and, directly after that, frees you from the depressive darkness. A book full of provocative ideas and exercises that will awaken your inner light. A remarkable show of autonomous thinking."

Lucas Derks PhD, social psychologist, author and developer of Mental Space Psychology

"When I received a platinum record 3 years ago for my contribution to the number one hit-song 'Take Your Time Girl' I was in the middle of a dark period of my life. All the success and even the celebratory drink with Goedele Liekens didn't change a thing about that; I took a taxi home, threw the platinum 'monster' in a corner and stayed in bed for a long time hiding under a black blanket...

Happiness is Depressing is frank, inspiring and written in a recognizable fashion. It makes a very complex theme understandable. Not just because of how Wassili writes in a patient and accessible way but also the layout and sharp quotes contribute to a deeper understanding. Wassili's own experiences as well as his findings build a credible bridge between science and practice.

This book has been a clear guide in my own search for self-knowledge. It specifically gave me 8 great insights as well as guidance and confirmation about self-doubts I was experiencing. Your method appeals to me, thank you!"
Patrick, Musician

"Incredibly inspiring book! Thanks!"
Edith Eeltink, coach and NLP Health certified

"Read *Happiness is Depressing* and... what an asset!"
Rilana Peeters

"This is not just another self-help book. No, this book might <u>actually</u> help you when you're suffering from a sombre mood or depression. *Happiness is Depressing* is written with substance and depth without becoming complicated or woolly. Our 'constant striving for happiness' can create a constant (unconscious) discontent or worse: depression. This book beautifully describes how we fall into that trap but also how to get out of it.

Wassili knows how to get to the essence of depression in an extremely clear and knowledgeable fashion <u>and</u> he offers a method to free yourself from it. Our mental processes as well as the depression are reframed. *Happiness is Depressing* is specific and practical with lots of exercises. This approach works because it is based on psychologic scientific knowledge but goes beyond the DSM. It actually exposes the many limitations regular psychology faces. Psychologists should read this book! Highly recommended!"
Barbara Le Noble

"Worth every penny!"
Zita Dusa

"Dear Wassili, I just finished your 3rd book and enjoyed it immensely <u>and</u> learned a lot from it. *Happiness is Depressing* came in very handy while working with a client with 'Climate induced isolation'."
Margot t Hart

"Wassili's personal story gives you the comforting feeling that you do not have to feel ashamed. One of the client cases he describes gave me a complete insight into my own situation and the cause of the tension I was experiencing. Insights he offers into 'our' way of thinking about happiness and trying to stop wanting to 'BE' happy are some of the pearls in this very nice book. Thank you Wassili."
Karim Ispahani

Wassili Zafiris

Happiness
is
Depressing

WAAS Publications

Imprint

WAAS Publications

Amsterdam
info@wassilizafiris.nl
www.wassilizafiris.nl

First edition: July 2019
Copyright © 2019 Wassili Zafiris
Author: Wassili Zafiris
Textual advice: Nienke van Oeveren
Editors: Tessa Jol and Aranka van der Pol
Final editor: Linda Rooijmans
Printing: PoD
Cover design: Magosja Turkawski
Cover illustration: Magosja Turkawski
Interior Design: Coco Bookmedia
Interior Layout: Coco Bookmedia
Translation: Gert Arts

ISBN: 9789090320427
NUR: 770

Originally published in Dutch in 2016 as *Geluk is Deprimerend* by
WAAS Publications, Amsterdam

Disclaimer
The methods described in this book have been found to be consistently gentle and transformational when tested on myself, and many hundreds of clients and workshop participants from 2008 on. As with any personal development book, readers are advised to use their own best judgement in using the methods provided. For those working with significant life issues (abuse, trauma, suicidal thoughts, severe depression), or in the event of any concern about wether or how to use the methods for yourself, we recommend contacting a skilled professional who is thoroughly trained in these methods. The information presented in this book is offered to you as a service. By reading this book you agree that you are responsible for any results of your decisions and actions relating to your use of the information presented. It is advised to consult a specialist when one experiences depressed thoughts and or feelings.

Contents

PART 3 ZEST FOR LIFE

Foreword by Tim Hallbom

I first met Wassili over 20 years ago while I was teaching at NLP University in Santa Cruz, California. I easily connected with him. Wassili asked me to review a book that he had written. I was pleased to do so as the book is about happiness, which is a subject that often comes up in the trainings that I conduct around the world, and in my coach practice.

Wassili has spent years exploring happiness both as a personal journey and as a professional coach working with all kinds of people who are hoping to be happier. He has studied the concept extensively and has a fun and (sometimes) irreverent style that makes this book both an easy read, and valuable one.

Many years ago, when I was learning to be a psycho-therapist, the focus of therapy was always on some kind of client psychopathology or problem. In the past couple of decades however, there's been a much greater emphasis on helping well-functioning people become happier and more successful. There are a number of books and programs about happiness and how you can achieve it. This book takes a somewhat different approach than most. Instead of pursuing happiness for its own sake, *this book will guide you in an incredibly self-aware and meaningful way of creating a happier more fulfilling life in a practical "how-to-do-it manner".*

This *really is a good book* because Wassili goes into depth about what happiness is, what it is not, and where it comes from. He shares both his own personal journey in trying to achieve it and lots of wisdom and information from sages and scientists studying the subject. Moreover, he gives you a number of ways to explore your own happiness. He also points out pitfalls that can occur through the pursuit of happiness that may actually leave you feeling more on the depressed side.

As you read your way through both the happiness and depression sections of the book, you will find a number of self-assessments that you can take. If you will you actually do them, you will make some useful self- discoveries and gain valuable insights about yourself. *You will begin to create an inner map for having true happiness.* In his final section of the book, *Zest for Life*, Wassili offers you tips and techniques and questionnaires that can guide you on a journey towards happiness.

We live in a culture in our modern world where there are a lot of signs and signals that say you should really strive for happiness. It is interesting that in the late 1990s M. Scott Peck wrote in his book, *The Road Less Traveled*, that most of us are conditioned to think that we are supposed to be happy, and if we are not happy then there is something wrong with us. In *this* book, you will find that the pursuit of happiness won't create the happiness that you want, rather it is finding the value and meaning in life and having a deeper understanding of you and your own process that is really going to make the difference in giving you a sense of fulfillment and true happiness.

One of the things I like best about Wassili's book, is that rather than offering a lot of "shoulds", he gives you practical how-to skills, tips and techniques for deeper self-understanding and greater happiness. As a coach and former therapist, many of the clients that I have seen are seeking some kind of counseling for them to become happier people. *This is a self-help book that can actually deliver in that regard.*

One area that Wassili explores is the impact of your self-talk and dialog on your ongoing experience. As an advanced Neuro-Linguistic practitioner and developer, Wassili makes explicit the fact that the words you say to yourself and others create your ongoing experience in life. This can be very subtle. For example, I had a client recently who said she needed to work hard on a relationship with her fiancé. Notice when you say the words "work hard" what images come to mind. Contrast that with "I want to improve my relationship with my fiancé". She had felt discouraged and unhappy about the prospects of "working hard" on the relationship. But she began to feel enthusiastic about what she could do to "improve my relationship". If you listen to your own internal dialog as Wassili suggests. You will discover your own words, phrases and thoughts that take you down the rabbit hole of unhappiness and resistance versus creativity, joy and enthusiasm for life.

All in all, I believe that you will discover ways to be a happier person when you read this book, think things through, employ the tips, techniques and processes that Wassili offers you.

Tim Hallbom
International NLP Trainer and Developer
Co-Founder NLP and Coaching Institute of California
Co-Author - *Beliefs: Pathways to Health and Well-Being,
Powerful Questions and Techniques for Coaches and Therapists,
NLP: The New Technology of Achievement*

Foreword by Dr Hein de Jong

Wassili Zafiris took a gamble by asking me to write an introduction for his book *Happiness is Depressing*. After all, I am a psychiatrist that has treated depressed people for many decennia. Most of the time with a combination of psychoanalysis and medication.

We met, Wassili and I, when he had just finished his book and I was writing my first novel. Two writers seated at a long table in France. I read Wassili's book in one breath then, and now read it a second time. We were both touched by the tremendous increase of depression in the world.

Wassili had become curious about his own experience with depressed feelings. Feelings that he at first did not recognize. In my family, depression is more common and has been a clear motivation for me to become a psychiatrist. We agreed quickly. Not all people with depression need medication, let alone psychotherapy. That would be impossible by any medical standard anyway. What to do then? In a time when there was confusion about the diagnosis of mental problems there was a clear need for order. A machete was needed to clear the way in the jungle. That's how the DSM classification system came into being. Psychiatry has moved 50 years ahead since then and we ourselves have walked *into the machete*. The path to clarity has led to a parcelled-out area with 350 diagnosed mental illnesses now, as opposed to 112 then. Frances, who led the composition of the DSM IV has been very clear about the fact that the DSM classification system has gone too far. *It has become a diagnosis bible and landed in the hands non-clinicians.* This could be due to refined diagnostics, as well as to misuse by the pharmaceutical industry. The sad consequence of this money abusing machine is that it has not led to a better treatment of the depressive client. Form has outstripped content.

So, what about Wassili's story? He states that from *within the dark room* that holds the client captive, if given the proper attention and interventions, an opening to the light can be found once again. The machete we run into is actually the repression of the complex moods we call depression. A living dynamic vision on the human condition of people with these problems has become a rigid system of diagnostics with an impaired vision of what it means to live in a dark room and what to do about that. Just like the fact that depression has become a fixed state so has happiness become an implicit demand in our lives instead of an adventurous ride. When we are down, we do not know our past anymore nor do we experience the opportunities of the future. We, because this can happen to all of us, will shape an inner world of sombre subjective experiences. Wassili is not interested in a diagnosis, he gets to work with his private clients and groups; and with the right attention depressed clients come out of their dark rooms. *This is a manual to find light again when feeling down and a learning manual for professionals.* Prevent and resolve loneliness, help them to get a realistic self-image, and teach them how to deal with setbacks. Make sure their inner world (or 'landscape' as Wassili calls it) does not remain static. Learn how to find strength and creativity in the depressed state, a state that is often a different name for mourning and unachievable assumptions. In this, psychoanalysis and Wassili's method find each other, each with their own target audience, but the latter is by far the biggest.

Dr H. de Jong psychiatrist-psychoanalyst

Author of *Onder de Hemel (Beneath the Heavens)*, 2019 and *Een psychoanalytische studie van poëzie (A psychoanalytic study of poetry)*, 2015

Preface

You are opening this book for good reason. Maybe you feel dissatisfied, are in low spirits or want to help somebody who is troubled by them... Depression? I never thought it would befall me...

The past ten years I have examined what we know about happiness and depression and how in the course of time we have come by this knowledge. Surprising insights have originated from this, and I share them with you by writing this book. These discoveries have led to new ideas and ways of finding happiness.

Writing *Happiness is Depressing* proved to be an enormous challenge. In the end, I have rewritten it three times and I have had to cope with many setbacks. I can truthfully say that the last year was tough because I devoted every free hour to my book. My family more often missed me than saw me. The last few months my four-year-old daughter asked me quite often: 'Daddy, isn't your book almost finished? Are we then going to play again?' There was a period in my life when, under this kind of pressure, I would have become low-spirited myself. What's more, I have been depressed myself. Not this time, though. And that is definitely due to what I have discovered about happiness and depression.

Depression is a highly charged phenomenon. There aren't many people who are open to really listening to depressed people. Yet I would like to advise everyone to get curious about the perception and experience of depression because it gives you a lot of clues about happiness in life by and large.

In this book, I frequently make use of the original definitions of words like happiness and depression. I recognize that everybody has their own view on them. Definitions change in the course of time. Sometimes an original definition doesn't resemble the modern definition of a word anymore. Surprisingly, the meaning of a word in people's perception often changes a lot less. My investigation into the original meaning of a number of words has given me a lot of insight into what it means to be happy and depressed.

By way of illustration, I have added examples from my practice. I have been so fortunate as to counsel thousands of people and therefore have at my disposal many stories illustrating how happy enterprising people get depressed all the same, and, with the right counselling, can create happiness in a new way. A few of these stories I have written down, hoping they are going to help you find the road to lasting happiness. All the names you come across in this book are fictitious, except mine.

Of course, I don't have a monopoly on wisdom. What I do know is that the method which has resulted from my research has not only yielded fresh ideas but has also proved to be effective with depressed persons. Therefore, this book is not only surprising and inspiring, but also critical; and it stimulates you to get cracking. That isn't always easy. Sometimes you really have to set to work at full tilt in order to discover the pearls that are hiding in your subconscious.

Through writing *Happiness is Depressing* I have learnt a lot about acceptance, connection, love, self-respect, resilience and happiness. It's my wish that you are going to find out just as much about yourself and lasting happiness as I have.

Introduction

In our success culture, striving for happiness has become a given. *Who doesn't just want to be happy?* Every day we are submerged in happiness messages. We long for a steady happy feeling. All the same, striving for happiness doesn't only have nice implications. Our quest for happiness, success, better and finer appears to be leading to a chronic feeling of dissatisfaction and even depression in an ever-expanding group of people.

Gloominess is found in several degrees: from 'I'm just not feeling quite all right' to 'I've had enough of it.' People who don't feel quite all right seldom call themselves depressed because they just can't explain their feelings. For people who are despondent, life has even lost all colour and meaning. With self-help books, gurus, courses, coaches, psychologists and finally even with psychiatrists we try to get happiness in our lives. To no avail. Because we are looking for the wrong...

This book has been written for people who just want to be happy *and* for people to whom happiness seems a utopia because gloom has become their everyday state of mind. Are you experiencing pessimistic and depressive thoughts or feelings? Do you feel down, lonely or overwhelmed? You'll want to read this book because it will give you understanding and a means to transform the darkness and find light. This book offers you guidance, support *and* coaches you to zest for life.

Happiness is Depressing is also a manual for coaches, therapists and counsellors. It is written from the perspective of the client as well as the coach, providing you with essential knowledge about the mindset of depression and how it comes into existence. *Happiness is Depressing* also offers the means to help shape zest for life for depressed and other clients. The insights in this book will give you a deeper understanding of how our way of thinking shapes our reality. On top of that you can use the new and advanced techniques directly in your daily practices. *Happiness is Depressing* can be read as a coaching journey with a sombre client. Ultimately this is the story of how the experience of a coach leads to the investigation and transformation of depression.

The essence of happiness

Happiness and unhappiness have everything to do with each other, maybe even more than you might suspect at first sight. In order to be happy, we have to wonder anew what happiness is, so as to obtain a clear picture of what we are aiming at. This book's goal is to de-sombre completely and to clarify why some of us are just not quite happy. We are going to find happiness.

Happiness is Depressing presents a holistic view on happiness and depression. It delves into various aspects, such as the impact of advertising and marketing on how we think about happiness, the words that lucky devils and unlucky devils use themselves, the medical approach of depression and a new view on how to experience the joy of living, and more. Also, I share my personal story: How, in a few months' time, I got from a stable, happy life into a depression. I will narrate how this understanding dawned on me and why I found it so difficult to extricate myself from the misery.

The issues of this book taken together create a new whole. A new outlook on how to get out of the gloomy darkness and find happiness once more. You are going to discover what happiness really means and will be handed the instruments to lead a more satisfying life. You are going to learn how to rebuild your hope of change. You will see that bright spots are to be found in the darkness and how you can embrace yourself as you are. You will get the feeling that you are part of your family, friends and even life, that you do belong. You are going to learn how you can transmute the significance of adversity and that you, too, can be lucky. The door to new opportunities will open and you will relearn how to enjoy your life, even though at present that seems to be a long way off.

Happiness, depression and zest for life

Happiness is Depressing is split up into three parts with separate themes: Happiness, Depression and Zest for Life. In the first two parts, you are presented with a new framework for happiness and depression. In the last part, *ZEST FOR LIFE*, I take you along, step by step, from darkness to light. From discontent and dejection to zest for life and the joy of living. By means of seven exercises, I help you get rid of low spirits and present you with an approach that enables you to experience happiness and to keep doing so. All parts together form the guide to lasting happiness. The first two parts are mainly informative and inspiring, the third part zeroes in on getting to work and experiencing stuff. If you are no reader and would rather get going straight away, you can take up the exercises of *ZEST FOR LIFE* right away.

In the first part, *HAPPINESS*, you are going to discover how important happiness has become in our daily life, but also how our striving for it has become a happiness enemy, and even appears to lead to depression. Our happiness culture has unintentionally brought about a taboo on failing, and that we are chiefly oriented towards positive emotions. Oddly, this leads to fewer instead of more feelings of happiness. You are going to discover what the language of happiness is and how our use of language can make us happy or miserable, and which definition of happiness will considerably increase your chances of a happy life.

In the second part, *DEPRESSION*, I give you a whole new view of what depression is, how it comes into being and how so many people can stay stuck in it. I show you what is currently known about depression and how the medical point of view gives answers in a limited degree about what depression is ('depression is a disorder') and what to do about it. I will uncover the assumptions that lie at the bottom of our present approach of dejection and will show how inaccurate and obstructive they are. You are going to learn the difference between the symptoms of depression and what someone in a depression experiences *inside*. You are taken along, as it were, in the inner landscape of depression in order to discover how depression gives rise to inner darkness. This landscape not only gives us new insights into what it means to be depressive but also into what has to be done to find happiness.

In the third and last part *ZEST FOR LIFE*, I am your guide in exploring your inner landscape. This part is a manual full of exercises to find once more the light from within the inner darkness. Among other things, we travel past happy and less happy to low-spirited and depressed in order to get answers to the question: 'How to get happy again when feeling down?' And how are you going to find real happiness when you aren't completely happy? By means of seven exercises, I teach you how in the darkness you can shine light once more. You are going to learn the latest change techniques, based on ten years of research, to uncover and change your inner world step by step. Ultimately you will learn in this part how to really experience zest for life and the joy of living.

My own search started when I became conscious of the fact that I was stuck in an inner world. By some whim of fate, I stumbled across a bright spot in that world. That bright spot opened the door to writing this book. This book is about how your door can again be set ajar and can stay that way, about how you can become happy in your life. Happy in a lasting manner.

My story

I never thought to get so down as to label myself as depressive. And yet it happened. In my case, this was extra bizarre since as a coach I know a lot about how to think purposefully, create solutions and how to change obstructive thoughts, feelings and beliefs. One of the reasons it is so wonderful to receive training in coaching is that you can try out all the change processes on yourself. In the years before I felt so down, I had done that endlessly, with a wealth of marvellous results. All the same, years later I merely felt wretched, dissatisfied, empty and dull. I could very well explain these feelings but didn't take any initiative to change my frame of mind. Nor could I define what was the matter with me; it was a weird, maybe even a surrealistic experience. This episode was the immediate cause for writing this book, because I realized that it was almost impossible to understand my experience, not only for people around me but also for myself. One of the things that astonished me most was my utter apathy; I stood by, watched and let it happen. I had the best toolbox one could think of for solving problems and didn't even open it...

For fifteen years I had already had a successful coaching and training business. I travelled all over the world, dined with successful entrepreneurs and sportsmen, and helped teams work together a lot better. I was busy, very busy, but that was nice and inspiring. I taught at several institutions and coached as many individuals as possible with all kinds of (life) questions. I had an awkward but happy relation (yes, it is possible) and after eight years we would finally live together in a newly bought house. Within a few months, my life was changing on several levels and I became depressive, seemingly overnight. Of course, it didn't happen that fast, so let's go back to the beginning...

In 2006 I had an accident. After a discussion with my girlfriend Lara, I decided to go sporting for a while on my racing bike. I did that a lot and, similarly, this Tuesday in August:

It's nice and warm and I put on a brisk spurt. Although I am in the middle of the town I am rapidly racing at full blast and heading at great speed for a crossing. I see that the crossing is completely empty, the light changes to orange, a look once more to the left, don't see any traffic and throw my weight on the pedals.

And then, suddenly, from out of nowhere there is a car. I brake with all my strength. Miraculously, I manage to bring the bike to a full stop a few centimetres before I hit the car, but, due to my high speed, I am catapulted over my bike. In full flight, I am hit on the head by the car. I glide for metres through the air and land on the ground with a thud. Silence!

I feel something is out of order and one thought shoots through my mind: no panic, Wassili, you can do that later. A woman comes running and I see the tears rushing to her eyes. 'Don't move!' The ambulance arrives quickly, just like Lara who had been drawn to the tumult and sees me being hoisted into a neck brace. Panic everywhere, in a hurry to the local hospital. I can feel my legs and can move my arms but can hardly open my mouth because the bone protuberance of one of my vertebrae touches my lower jaw when I open my mouth. The pain is hard to bear, and nobody knows what to do. Until a doctor hammers things back with a small hammer and a chisel. Ah, that is a relief. Then the doctor says: 'You may go home sir, you may consider yourself fortunate.' With those words Lara and I take a taxi home.

After a few days' rest I try to pick up the thread. Lara is sweet and looks after me. One day, all of a sudden, she is standing with her coat on in front of me. 'Come on, hurry up,' she says. 'Hurry up what?' I ask her. She looks at me strangely, as if something is not right. 'What do you mean', she says 'We decided just now to go for a stroll, didn't we?' I sincerely have no inkling what she is talking about and simply don't understand it. In a kind of daze, she takes off her coat and leaves it at that.

I notice that in the following days my memory is failing me more and more. I accept that as a given of the collision. I'm getting a bit more worried when in the succeeding weeks I have trouble speaking. I can only find words with difficulty and sit somewhat apathetic on the couch much of the time. After a few weeks, I decide to start working again and pack my things to give a training in a nearby town. That night in the local bar I'm preparing for the following training day when out of the blue I'm seeing only half of the huge Heineken signboard. I think: This isn't right. As a one-time neurological physiotherapist, I realized its possible severity. In a local hospital they do a peripheral vision test and part of the visual field of my left eye appears to have vanished. The doctor observes: 'This is not good: We're going to examine you further.'

Many check-ups later the hypothesis is that my brain stem has got a blow, which should explain all these phenomena. With an unworried mind, I resume my activities at half power.

In the meantime, my relation has run into stormy weather. We were already having discussions before my accident, but they are on the increase, which is alarming, seeing that next month we are receiving de key of our new build house.

On my birthday, 30 November, we decide to break up. My expectation for the future is scattered. However, because I am not feeling all right it doesn't quite get through to me. Moreover, I have a thriving business of my own and in three weeks' time, the builders will be in the shell of my house. An intensive period is beginning. Early in the morning, I go to my new house to instruct the workmen before immersing myself in my work (and doing the administration after that) and then go to my house once more to have a look at what has been done and plan the next day. Late in the evening, I roam websites for advice, doorknobs, primers and skirting. For days on end, this goes on and on, for weeks on end, until a note drops into my letterbox. Would I see the doctor once more?

As a matter of course, I report to the neurology department, but I don't appear to belong there; I have to report to oncology. Oncology, I don't understand but report dutifully. The door swings open and a nice lady looks at me. She has a look in her papers and says: 'A tumour factor has been found in your faeces; we are going to investigate if you have cancer.' I wasn't in high spirits anyway, but this was just too much. Six uncertain weeks lie ahead. When I report again to the doctor there is another oncologist. He has a look in the papers, reads them all closely and says: 'We haven't found anything, but this first outcome can also be positive in case of inflammation, so probably it was that.

Instead of tumbling from my chair with astonishment, I shake the doctor's hand and cycle home in a daze. Relieved but confused I resume where I had left off. Meanwhile, things begin to go against me with the building of the house. My contractor is taking me in and one thing after the other misfires. A wall collapses, the bath that has just been built appears to leak quite a bit, stuff vanishes... I feel very much alone and start withdrawing more and more. I am literally alone, for that matter. My mother died a few years ago, and my father lives abroad. Weeks go by, I'm overcome with exhaustion and feel worse by the day. In a kind of desperate effort, I go to work too in the house. Friends are busy, so I have to get my stuff out of my old house myself and surrender it properly...

I keep doing my coaching work. I'm good at it, anyway. It is the moment of the day that I feel more or less all right. I can apparently rely on my knowledge and experience to such an extent that, even in this situation, I function excellently. I'm getting clients of a kind I used to have fewer of, that is to say people who were down, saw no way out. At those moments I think: Ah, it's the same with me. However, in spite of all my knowledge and experience, I'm doing nothing at all about it. Strangely enough, it doesn't occur to me.

Summer has come and while the sunbeams are shining through my window, I make up my mind: 'If I go on feeling like this for another day, I'll do myself in.' I'm feeling so bad that this *decision really is a very positive decision, a very clear decision. Not a call for attention, but a fact.*

Elize, a friend I know from one of my trainings, visits me more and more regularly. I don't see why, but she is quite pleasant company. 'It's nice you're here, but you shouldn't expect anything from me', I tell her straight away. She obviously senses where I stand and agrees. She has a very joyous mindset and outlook on life, and I like that, from a distance anyway. 'Let's go and walk for a bit in the woods tomorrow. That's good for you and nice, too', Elize proposes. I hear those words and rationally grasp that what she says is true. Having a good time outside, with her, walking, nature, all nice things, but these things just stay merely things. I have no contact with them. I understand what she's saying but am totally unable to feel its meaning any more. As if what she is saying still exists in the world outside me, but not anymore in the world inside me. I hear her out, don't say anything about it and dutifully accompany her the next day.

A friend has come to help me sand the floor and gives me a look. 'Well, it's just heavy now, but in a month your house will be finished and you'll be enjoying your new house and will be meeting lovely new folks. Come on, buddy, tomorrow is another day', he tries to cheer me up. I hear him out and understand what he says, but not a thing of what he is saying resonates. Anyway, I am much too tired and don't see any reason to explain to him what I am going through inside. I haven't got the energy for it, but it doesn't matter either to my way of feeling. I leave it at that and we carry on with the jobs we were doing.

Going to bed that night I look in the mirror and am shocked. I have always been a sportsman and have been very fit all of my adult life. Now I am looking in the mirror and see too fat a man in front of me, his belly bulges and his former muscles have been replaced by a thin layer of body fat. I'm shocked by this image and literally say to myself: 'This isn't me.'

In spite of all this stuff, there is nothing in me that so much as gets the idea to do something about it, to find a solution or to use my experience to take a close look at myself. There is a kind of total apathy with regard to my state of mind. And tomorrow, pooh, oh yes, tomorrow it's going to be a lot better.

On a bright day in September, a client visits me for the first time. A nice fellow, I have known him for years, since I gave a training on teams in his business. We greet each other cordially and he starts his story by telling me that he has had a problem for five years or so. Each and every time he is thinking of his ex-girlfriend a kind of gloominess comes over him and this is bothering him so much that he wants to talk with somebody who knows about these things. He explains that his ex abruptly broke off their engagement at a friend's wedding party and that after that he hasn't had a decent talk with her. When he sees her at the house of mutual friends, he feels huge anger surging, but as he doesn't know what to make of those feelings or how to handle them, he swallows them.

'In what way is that a problem?', I ask him. 'Now, my problem is that I haven't had a relationship since then and that this doesn't work anymore one way or another. I do meet other girls but it doesn't work out or something', John explains. After a thorough talk, we start formulating a goal, and with that, we conclude our first talk. 'See you in two weeks', I say at the end. Though the talk went well, I didn't have the feeling that we had already reached the kernel of his story.

A few talks further and after the usual interventions, I think we're not really progressing. All sorts of small things turn up which to me are becoming a kind of thread in his story. Among other things, he had indicated that, true enough, he did have friends, but felt lonely all the same; that, one way or another, he definitely wanted to stay indoors, and, if things went against him, he would rather hide that from the outside world. However, what I found the most interesting was that, after all, he didn't do the tasks I gave him, while, with a big smile, he said each and every time that he was surely going to carry them out. 'Yes, it kind of doesn't come about; I do intend to do it, but, don't know,' he apologizes.

*On the spot, I decide to do something new and ask him if he
would like to make a list of symptoms. 'What do you mean?'
John asks. I explain: 'Well, a list of all the symptoms you have
now.'*

*At that moment I'm struggling myself with what precisely I want
to ask. My first question is: 'When you think of tomorrow, what
happens?' In a reflex he says: 'I have to see a customer.'
I repeat the question: 'When you think of tomorrow, suppose
you can do something pleasant, a friend asks you to come along
with him to your favourite bar, what happens inside you then?'
'Nothing', he answers resolutely.
'What do you mean by 'nothing'?'
Minutes pass and he is pondering deep inside: 'Tomorrow is
nothing to me, tomorrow doesn't exist, or something like that.'
Fascinated by that utterance I continue with my next question:
'How do you view yourself?'
Question after question follows and John answers all the
questions I think up on the spot.
I carefully peruse the list with answers and read all the
symptoms to him, one after the other. In my head, each and
every symptom he mentions resonates: Shit, that's me! All of a
sudden a sinking feeling overcomes me: 'F*ck, I am depressed!'*

*As if the steel chair I'm sitting in is tightening around me, that's
how I begin to grasp my predicament. All the symptoms together
create the inescapable understanding that I am depressed.
While I am recovering from the shock, I once more read him the
symptoms he mentioned and ask: 'How would you call this?'
He looks at me upset and says: 'F*ck, I am depressed!' He, too,
feels a shock going through him, visibly. I keep silent about my
experience and we finish the session and decide to meet again
the next week.*

*During the days after this talk, I actually did not only feel a
shock, but also a release. That shock slowly registered with me;
it matters quite a lot, depressed. It doesn't only say something
about the problem you have, but also about what kind of person
you are, what apparently you can and can't handle, and what
will other people make of it? My God, how am I going to explain*

*this? But also other thoughts like: Yes, you are in a tight corner,
you will only with difficulty get out of this, this is heavy shit.
Apparently, at the back of my mind I had all sorts of ideas about
what it means to be depressive and what is to be expected then.
Virtually all those ideas were quite serious and grave, so my
future, dark as it was, was not going to brighten up.*

*Release I felt as well; so far I had been in the middle of a feeling,
and that feeling (with the matching thoughts) had me in its
power. I was at its mercy. For the first time I understood myself
and this insight set something free in me, as if I was given point
of departure of a kind.*

*Now I was still terribly down, that hadn't been altered at all.
I didn't magically get proactive about my situation, everything
was the same, but something had changed as well. I kept this
to myself and, moreover, I was still in half a house with a
bathroom that had been pulled down and whose contractor had
gone on holiday for a month, just like that, without telling me
how I could reach him. So much for being on friendly terms with
a contractor...*

*I still wasn't having any thoughts about my own situation,
but I was thinking about John, for I didn't have a really good
idea how to handle this effectively. Of course, I had learned
about depression, but what are you going to do with depression?
What was my next step going to be in the coaching? The list of
symptoms was big, and everything looked important. What aim
are we going to pursue? I didn't know but was curious about it.*

*After I hadn't been able to find much of substance about it in the
literature, I thought I was being smart by searching something
about depression on the internet the day before John was to
come again. One commonplace after the other passed by. The
Diagnostic and Statistical Manual of Mental Disorders (DSM)
of the American Psychiatric Association is central in this. The
DSM is the handbook in which our mental aberrations are
neatly classified, and it is used to determine which psychological
problem you do or don't have. The lists of symptoms in it are
so general that it looks like everybody has the symptoms of*

depression. I racked my brain over whether depression would be an illness, read the DSM once more and searched all over the net, until I thought of the following: When I'm coaching people I always go towards some goal or other. After some searching on the internet, I entered 'the opposite of depression' because in coaching you are keen on having a goal to work towards and I realized I didn't know what it was. I pressed the mouse and, to my utter amazement, roughly two words came along again and again. One: 'elevation', e.g. lifting the shoulders, and two: 'mania', the pathological state of mind which is accompanied by excitement, irritability and confusion.

My heart began to beat faster and, at the same time, I was left totally flabbergasted. Could it be that there doesn't exist a goal when you are depressed? Could it be that we only know how to define the problem? Could it be that we are so deeply conditioned that in case of depression we exclusively think of the problem because we haven't learned to specify what you are heading for when you are depressive? If this is true, would that explain why I had been completely passive all those months? We may not yet have brought up for discussion what the real solution for depression is.

What are people who are depressed looking for? Happiness? I wasn't looking for anything. Nor was client John. I was wondering: What is happening in me when I think of tomorrow? I took the time to ask myself this question and the only thing that emerged in me was a black nothing. Not a single association with tomorrow. I understood the concept of tomorrow, but, in my inner world, tomorrow was just a story, a word of another person. All of a sudden, I understood my lack of understanding when friend Elize came along, once more understanding and cheerful, and began to talk pleasantly about a nice walk with her later on. Then I often said: 'Good idea', but that nice walk later on didn't exist for me. Nor did I have any idea how to explain this to her. That's why I didn't even try. And when people with the best intentions said: 'Cheer up buddy, it will be better soon', or 'Soon all sorts of nice things will be waiting for you', and more of those well-intentioned boosts, then those well-intentioned boosts meant nothing to me.

It was to me as if they were talking about an extra-terrestrial entity that no one had ever seen and that no one knew what it looked like. In my inner world, there was no later. And when 'later' doesn't exist anymore, what are you going to do? Not very much, in my case. Being happy if you are not, is also a matter of later. I really did want to be happy again, and said so too, but deep inside this was a vain hope. If 'later' does not even exist anymore, becoming happy is totally out of reach. Then happiness is an extra-terrestrial entity that no one has ever seen and no one knows what it looks like.

Introduction part 1
Happiness

The quest for a happy and meaningful life makes one
thing clear: it not easy to accomplish and each moment of
happiness seems a fleeting experience. The moment you
are experiencing it, it's gone again. There are days it seems
as if the whole world is trying to teach us something about
happiness and being happy. It is an everlasting pursuit.

What if our search for happiness is a mistake? What if
it is a misrepresentation, a gimmick of our mind, which
sends us in the wrong direction. What if the whole notion
of happiness is a deception? Suppose that our search for
happiness, meaning and fulfilment is really one of the
reasons for our being stuck, and even of the continuous
rise of the number of cases of depression in our society? I
will show you that we are pursuing the wrong aim and that
we have to redefine happiness, not only in order to be able
to experience more happiness in our lives, but also to be
able to change dejection.

On the one hand, our striving after happiness seems a
survival mechanism, on the other hand, a slick advertising
ploy to ensure that we keep the economy going. In the part
Happiness I show what I mean by that and why we are so
eager to pursue happiness in our lives. But also, how our
wish for happiness can cause great problems. Without us
being aware of that every day, our pursuit of happiness is
a fear-driven endeavour, in the course of which we have
collectively developed a taboo on failing. Doing so, we
try to avoid as much as possible emotions like fear, anger,
grief. Doing business, too, is interlarded with the pursuit
of happiness. However, there it is indicated, and given
emphasis, by terms like 'success', 'constantly improving'
and 'achieving'. Our pursuit of happiness has blinded us
in a certain way, and, as will become clear in Chapter 3
The language of happiness, our formulation of 'happiness'
plays an important role in our pursuit of happiness. In the

end you will discover that we have misdefined happiness, as a result of which we may set our sights on a feeling of happiness, but seldom experience it for a long time. That's why I define happiness once again in the last chapter. This is extremely important, for if you don't see clearly what you are looking for, it's hard to find.

1.
The happiness culture as enemy

We live in a happiness culture, everything around us is aimed at happiness. Daily we are told what it will bring you to be happy, beautiful and successful. Advertisement, TV and marketing cleverly take advantage of this and tell us how and what to do in order to have the best possible aura. Our school system teaches us that success will lead to the ultimate happiness. Every personal-development programme and TV programme, virtually everything aims at finding, uncovering and activating happiness. And let's be honest, who does not want to be happy? From more friends to better health, happiness helps us in everything. However, there are drawbacks to our going after happiness and success. One might call them the enemies of happiness, and, paradoxically, it is our wish for happiness that is our enemy. In this chapter, I explain what I mean by this. But first I set the record straight on happiness.

Happiness is gold
Happiness is like the gold of life. Everybody wishes for it and once you have it you think you can deal with the world. In personal development, therapy and coaching, too, we generally go after happiness. For if you score that, what else is left to be wished for? If we could have converted it into shares, these shares would be worth gold. Human happiness is one of the most pursued experiences in life. Ask anyone what they long for and you will always find somewhere in the top five something like 'I want to be happy'. Bookshops are full of books about happiness, gurus promote their latest ideas and tenets of how to accomplish ultimate happiness in seven steps. Spiritual

teachers tell us to find roads to happiness within and without ourselves, and once in a while, a new idea comes along which catches the flame of happiness. Mindfulness and positive psychology are the latest fads. Psychologists, psychiatrists and researchers look into every aspect of happiness and find more hints than was ever believed possible. Every puzzle piece of happiness behaviour has been mapped. Journals and papers show us what a happy person looks like, how the happy couple behaves, how the ideal family should organize themselves, and the list goes on and on. Every aspect of our personal need for happiness is nourished in this manner.

Have you ever thought: If only I felt happy, then life would be way nicer? What do people spend the most money on? What does everybody travel far and wide for? Happiness is the emotion everybody wants to experience. Being happy is the most desired state of mind. Happiness is the key to everything.

The feasibility of happiness

Geneticists believe that fifty percent of our happiness experience is accounted for by our genes. So, if you have had a bit of luck, you have received from your parents the right mix of happiness genes, and for that reason alone you look happier. And though the geneticists are not clear about how they have come by this number, one can imagine that if you are, for instance, healthy (read: have the right genes) you can more easily feel happy than, for instance, your sick neighbour, who has just bad luck as far as his gene pool is concerned.

It turns out that only ten percent of our happiness experience is determined by our living conditions. Ten percent is really very little if you realize that it is exactly our living conditions we try to work on to be happier. We try to create a more prosperous life by a better income, a new title, or a wonderful idea you can conquer the market with, hoping that wealth will make us happier. What bad luck we have, though, when nearly all research shows that, for instance, more money doesn't make us happier. Money and happiness haven't got to do much with each other, unfortunately. The same applies to beauty. A pretty face and a good figure are absolutely helpful in getting relations, jobs, and life in general, but beauty in itself doesn't make us happier. Just think of Ken and Barbie, I'm not talking about the dollies, but about this man and woman who let themselves be sculpted, by means of plastic surgery, after their gurus, the dolls Ken and Barbie. One would think that their dream has come true after many operations, but after each surgery, a new disappointment has to be dealt with, all but achieved perfect beauty.

No, good looks don't make us happier. After all, you get used to anything. For years you can wake up in ecstasies next to the most beautiful man or woman, but according to psychologists, a moment will arrive that you think: Is this really it? Apparently, we adjust our expectations and that is *fatal* for our feeling of happiness, for instead of just going on to enjoy what we have, we always need to think the grass might be greener on the other side of the fence. Psychologists call this principle *hedonic adaptation.* Our adaptability catapults us into an infinite search for happiness.

However hard we do our best to improve our living conditions, in the end we won't get any happier thereby. Let's face it, ten percent is just a little bit better than a chance of a winning number in a lottery. Bizarre that, all the same, we pay so much attention to it. This is because we have the feeling that we can influence our living conditions, and from a lot of research it appears that the feeling of influence is very important to us.

If all our effort proves to be useless, is it then at all possible to experience more happiness in our lives? Shouldn't we rather quit pursuing happiness? According to neuroscientists our brain is designed for happiness.[1] Brain areas have been determined that have especially been designed to process positive emotions. From this it can be concluded that in a specific way we have a gift for a joyful and happy life.

Geneticists have also demonstrated that there is a depression gen and that those who've got this 5-HTTLPR gene have a higher chance to get depressive than people who haven't got this gene. Though about the impact of this gene, by and large, there is no consensus among scientists.[2]

Ultimate happiness

So, fifty percent of our experience of happiness is determined by our genes, ten percent by our living conditions. Then forty percent remains, which we may be able to influence ourselves. For this forty percent is determined by our way of thinking and behaving. When you realize what the advantages are of experiencing more feelings of happiness and you want to move a bit closer to a happier life, you would be stupid if you didn't bring all your attention to it.

In addition to the obvious fact that with a feeling of happiness you feel better, there are many more advantages: happy people are more social-minded, more energetic, kinder and more popular. They stand a better chance of getting married and staying married. They have a bigger social network and receive more social care when needed. Happy people are flexible and resourceful. They are better at managing people and negotiating and earn more. They have a stronger immune system, are physically healthier and live longer.

1   Morten Kringelbach en Kent Berridge, *The Neuroscience of Happiness and Pleasure*, PMC, US National Library of Medicine, juli 2011
2   https://en.wikipedia.org/wiki/5-HTTLPR

Advantages of being happy

In becoming happier, we not only boost experiences of joy, contentment, love, pride, and awe but also improve other aspects of our lives: our energy levels, our immune systems, our engagement with work and with other people, and our physical and mental health. In becoming happier, we bolster as well our feelings of self-confidence and self-esteem; we come to believe that we are worthy human beings, deserving of respect. A final and perhaps least appreciated plus is that if we become happier, we benefit not only ourselves but also our partners, families, communities, and even society at large. From: Lyubomirsky, Sonja. *The How of Happiness* (p. 26). Penguin Publishing Group. Kindle Edition.

Of course, these are things we all want. Surely you aren't going to say no to a terrific list like this one, are you? This is the ultimate, and yes, we all want this!

The downside of happiness

Yet there is something paradoxical the matter with happiness. Scientist and gurus agree in this case: The harder you try the further away happiness seems to be. Happiness is like sand, the harder you squeeze, the more it slips through your fingers.

If happiness is really so wonderful, why hasn't everybody got it already for a long time? Ever since antiquity people have written about it: Aristotle, Buddha, God, Robbins, Buffet. Everybody tries to hand us a piece of the puzzle. But why hasn't the ultimate happiness meditation, wisdom, or quite simply happiness pill, not yet been thought of and invented? If everything in and around us is oriented towards a happier life, why are we fighting so hard to be happy? The reason is that there are (unconscious) problems attached to our striving for happiness.

Recent research reveals that dangers, too, come with our inexhaustible pursuit of happiness. As will become apparent later in this book, there is a staggering relation between happiness seekers, their focus on themselves and the resulting feeling of loneliness and the growth of depression. Feeling happy can also lead to being less creative (think of the artist who can only create out of negative emotion, and not out of positive feelings). And in a number of cases feelings of happiness appear to be the cause of you being less able to connect to other people. It appears that the more store is set by feelings of happiness, the lonelier people can feel. Why, would you think? The answer is simple. People who value happiness highly, are generally more self-directed, even at the cost of contact with others.[3]

However, there are more downsides to our pursuit of happiness. Happiness seekers are often not the best goal setters. For being happy is a rather vague aim in itself. 'I just want to be happy', seems quite clear when you say it, but what are you talking about for heaven's sake? One thing is clear when it comes down to reaching targets: The vaguer the target, the more chances of disappointment.

Besides, happiness seekers often appear to have an awkward relationship with their other emotions. The happiness seeker is averse to feelings associated with failure, anxiety, grief and anger, as a result of which sound emotional intelligence is a long way off. Uncomfortable feelings have to be rubbed off as quickly as possible, and even before it is known what these feelings are about, they have been poured over with a kind of heavenly juice to pretend these emotions don't and didn't exist. So, our need for happiness returns again and again, and also the wish to go after it. The here and now is undervalued and the pot of gold at the end of the rainbow is made number one.

Happiology

The book *Flourish* by author and psychologist Martin Seligmann describes the problems the unremitting search for the positive, glad and successful is beset by. It is remarkable that Seligmann, of all people, comes up with this criticism, because in his earlier books he extols the joyful, positive and successful. He even states that he regrets the title of his worldwide bestseller *Authentic happiness* since his view on happiness in life has undergone a drastic change.

---

3   Iris Mauss, Maya Tamir, Craig Anderson, Nicole Savino, *Can Seeking Happiness Make People Happy? Paradoxical Effects of Valuing Happiness*, Emotion, August 2011

Seligmann realized that pursuing happiness might not bring with it all the profits he thought. He is annoyed at the endless recommending of happiness as the only and ultimate pursuit, which he jokingly calls *happiology*[4]: pursuing a constant experience of happiness, the need to continuously feel happy. Seligmann thought that the aim of personal development was to get as much satisfaction as possible out of life and to go for happiness. One of the examples he uses to illustrate that happiness cannot be our supreme pursuit, is the fact that childless couples feel happier than couples with children. The question that pops up is: 'Why is it then that people take children?' Apparently, the burden, the care and the possible relational stress that children bring with them, don't offset the caring feeling, being together and having a family, even if, due to this, the general feeling of happiness has to be adjusted downwards. Consequently, Seligmann argues that happiness can't be one of the most important motives in life. Currently, he says that we should go for well-being, the degree to which you can flourish.

Our mind misleads us. Success, chocolate, a pot with gold... Unconsciously, we make the weirdest assumptions about how to lead a happy life. For instance, quite a few happiness seekers think that you can find happiness, as if it were hidden or is waiting for you. Others believe that happiness can come your way if only you wish hard enough for it, or try long enough, for instance by wishing that you will win the lottery. Looking for happiness with these magical expectations about happiness at the back of your mind will not make your search for happiness an easy one, because you are quite often going to be disappointed. We suppose that things will work out. At any rate, our hope is placed in that and the business world joins in just as energetically.

---

4   Martin Seligmann is one of the most prominent psychologists of the twentieth century, the inventor of positive psychology and author of the bestseller Authentic Happiness.

'Be positive, optimistic and focussed on success: that is the modern mantra. But maybe you must learn to be a loser to find the real path to satisfaction.'

Oliver Burkeman

Failure not allowed

We live in a *'happy' culture*, in every fibre of our society. Our business world, as well, is interspersed with it. In Ann Arbor, in Michigan (U.S.) is a curious museum. It is a museum of failed products. In the sixties, the owner Robert McMath started collecting products that didn't catch on with the consumers (so not necessarily products that didn't work). He did this as a marketing man to start a reference database of a kind. In a few years, though, he had to move to a bigger accommodation, for what he hadn't realized is that most products companies make turn out to be flops! The failure rate of a product even proved to be ninety percent, and soon his premises were filled with consumer products that had gone wrong.

Even more interesting is the fact that a building with failures products has become a source of income for Robert. How? Strikingly many firms come along with their research and development departments to discover what they have made sometime in the past. Sorry? Firms that come along to discover what they have made sometime in the past? Yes, it looks like most firms don't keep a database of the products they have once made, and they often invent the same products dozens of times. The hunt for success is so great that they don't learn from their failures. Failed products are deleted from collective memory as quickly as possible to embark with renewed courage upon *the next big thing*. When in a few years the research teams are replaced with new people, all these people start with fresh courage... on the same products with often the same results. Failure is not allowed, and because failure is such a taboo and because only the most wonderful, most successful product is allowed to enter our collective consciousness, many millions are spent on ever the same things. Unbelievable, isn't it? Not quite, for we really do the same.

Behind our way of going for happiness and success, there is an assumption: that things will work out fine. This we are focussed on. Ever since the first philosophers, the opposite has been asserted. It is precisely our unparalleled exertion to feel happy or to want to accomplish objectives which makes us feel wretched, Oliver Burkeman says in his book *The Antidote: Happiness for People Who Can't Stand Positive Thinking*. Behind our pursuit of happiness, there is a deep-rooted uneasiness about uncertainty, insecurity and failure. This causes us to (unconsciously) sabotage our own plans.

Our opportunistic brain

Our focus on making sure that things go well seems to be installed in our brain. It turns out that our brain stores the chance of things going well bigger (literally in bigger images) than they are going to happen in actual fact. According to neuroscientists this comes in handy from an evolutionary perspective, because thereby we have gone on living and surviving; always keeping in mind that we have to go on and stay optimistic. It is an opportunistic trait of the brain which helps us, as a species, to survive.

There are various movements that employ this knowledge. Among other things, many visualization techniques have been developed in the world of personal effectivity, positive psychology, The Secret, neurolinguistic programming (NLP) et cetera. Visualizations, if performed correctly, can yield a lot, though in recent years dissenting opinions have been heard when it comes to positive visualizations. Apart from the fact that this opportunistic mechanism can disappoint us time and again with what actually becomes of our nice dreams, several experiments show that people who apply and practice positive visualizations, can, at last, lose their motivation to realize these dreamt-up objectives.

It is as if they have them already in their heads, due to which they lose their interest in having the dream become reality.[5]

Thinking in ideal pictures

In spite of these opportunistic features, we are fear-driven creatures and do everything to feel safe. Insecurity about our future is for many of us a very uneasy idea for which we often seek confirmation of the opposite. Usually, reassurance is the motto. 'Darling, it'll be alright, don't worry, what you are thinking is definitely not going to happen', we like to say to our loved ones and friends who are insecure and afraid. However, inadvertently reassurance can add to someone's fear and insecurity. The hidden message of reassurance actually is that it would be terrible if that future would come true.

IDEAL IMAGE

In my practice, a couple arrived that had already been quarrelling for ten years about seeming futilities. The last few years these arguments had become more vehement. Anne told me that she is really hurt by the fact that she and Eric have been quarrelling so much since the birth of their son ten years ago. The dream of having a family is daily scattered by an angrily running away Eric.

Eric, on the other hand, wants his wife back, as he calls it. For him the quarrels are about another ideal picture, that is to say, that he wants himself and his wife to be the centre of the family, and not 'the family'. 'I am married to you, and not the family', he snaps at Anna. The quarrels are always about the fact that life's reality and the ideal picture they have in their minds don't agree. To have to cope with the disappointment of a dreamt-up future not coming true seems to be more unbearable than the daily dose of quarrel.

5   Gabriele Oettingen, *Rethinking Positive Thinking*, 2014

We do everything to make our thought-up future real because, whatever the cost, we don't want to deal with the disappointment that it isn't going to become real. This might explain why people stay in bad relations or work situations because admitting that the happiness ideal is not coming true is experienced as unbearable. Unfortunately, about the only way of thinking we learn is thinking in ideal pictures. For that, you only need to watch tv.

Fear as a motive for happiness

How did our happiness images come into being? In the twentieth century, marketing and advertisement have rather chipped in with manipulating how we think about a happy life. It's a hundred-year-old advertisement secret: You map the fears people have for the sole purpose of thinking up a temporary solution for them. Because a new fear and consequently a new product must never be long in coming. A brilliant method to bring our happiness feeling to our attention and keep it there. What's so shrewd about good advertisement is that especially ultimate happiness is put in the centre of our attention. After all, without fear you are free to be optimally happy.

'Advertisement is based on one thing: happiness. And do you know what happiness is? Being free of fear.'

From *Mad Men, first instalment,* Don Draper

Do you know when the Hummer (that over-the-top big car of the American Army) became a (very) successful consumer product? Just after 9/11. The French anthropologist Clotaire Rapaille, who has advised companies like General Motors, Kellogg's and Philip Morris for more than thirty years, realized that by the attacks the 'reptile brain' of man had rushed into fear mode, and that this was the exquisite opportunity to sell ultimate personal safety. And it happened exactly that way. Twenty percent of American car sales consisted of SUVs and similar cars.

Advertising has long since started using emotions to advocate products. In 1916 Stanly B. Resor took over advertising agency J. Walter Thompson and began to advertise based on the latest knowledge about the human mind. Freud's knowledge and ideas became the guidelines of this agency, founded on the idea that the core of the modern consumer society boils down to creating fear, which is then offered a solution for. In this way, 'antibacterial' soap has arrived on our shelves. Bacteria are 'very dangerous' pathogens, and the way to feel carefree is to wash yourself and your children with antibacterial soap. Now it appears that the antibacterial effect is negligible in comparison with ordinary soap, that the antibacterial substances are not quite harmless and that, on the contrary, we need bacteria for a healthy life.[6] Yet, many people still buy antibacterial soap... and lots of other products with limited effectiveness which we believe we cannot do without, and which are all developed from the same thought. However, it's not only products that can make us feel happier, but also services like insurances, whereas, statistically, the dangers we can be insured for actually only happen to a very limited extent.

One fundamental fear we are confronted with, consciously and unconsciously, is rejection, not belonging. For this unbearable fear, wonderful 'solutions' are presented, like the latest phone, shoes, clothing and so on. Anything to belong. This is drilled into our children at an early age. Resor set the tone in the fifties with the girl Jane from the first Listerine advertisement. 'Jane is pretty, has a lovely

6   *Antibacterial soap with triclosan 'no better at killing germs'* – study, The Guardian, september 2015

figure, but men never stay long with her. Why? She has bad breath.'

Infinite effort

Hedonic adaptation, the realization that you get used to anything, is one of the greatest enemies of our happiness in life. An unconscious solution that people seem to use, in order not to get into a rut, is to keep assigning power to what you attach so much value to (and which gives you such strong feelings of happiness). You do this by thinking regularly that you could lose it. That fear brings all your attention back to your happiness object, leaving little or no opportunity for adjustment to feelings. Habituation is then compensated by the visualization of a fear scenario.[7]

We live in a world where everything is supposed to go all right. Being happy is the ultimate dream. Our brain encourages our pursuit of happiness by visualizing our experiences as large but as unspecific as possible, and does so against a backdrop of fear. We prefer to avoid negative emotions, and happy emotions we experience as many times more important than our less joyful ones. We erase our traces of failure and simply start once more time and again. Unfortunately, this endeavour is infinite, because once our fear is gone, we need a new fear (and a new product) to feel happy.

Summary

In our success culture, pursuing happiness has become a given. Our greatest fear is to lose our happiness. We are daily immersed in happiness messages. The fact that we are driven by fear is cleverly taken advantage of to keep us focused on temporary happiness by means of advertising and success visualizations. In business, success-oriented thinking has even led to a taboo on failure. Hedonic

---

7   That is exactly why Stoicism (originated several years after the death of Aristotle) suggested to visualize the worst scenario instead of the most beautiful: you will discover that this worst scenario does not match your reality. A stoic calm can then come over you.

adaptation ensures that we have to look for new happiness time and again. Our culture of happiness glorifies what is supposed to be successful and effective and supposed to make people happy.

All the same, striving for happiness doesn't only have nice implications. We appear to persistently make wrong assumptions about what makes us happy, like our living conditions, instead of adapting our way of thinking and behaviour. It also turns out that doing our utmost or buying a lottery ticket does not necessarily bring happiness closer. Our pursuit of happiness turns out to be our happiness enemy, for if you attach a certain value to happiness, it is more likely that you:

→ Are more often self-centred, which can lead to feelings of loneliness;

→ Are vague in your objectives, making it unclear what you are working towards, which causes you to have to deal with disappointments;

→ Have a worse relationship with the other emotions, such as sadness, anger and fear. You can then develop the feeling that you live at odds with these feelings, which can bring struggle and unrealistic expectations in relationships and with yourself;

→ Are very future-oriented, so that the 'now' is lost sight of.

All these factors determine your general well-being and can, without you being aware of it, slowly but surely create more darkness than you had thought possible.

Emotions play an important role in experiencing happiness. Your relationship with your emotions has so much impact on your feelings of happiness that it can stand in the way of your happiness. In the next chapter, you will learn how this works and especially how you can initiate other relationships with your emotions. So the light can shine again.

2.
Emotions and a happy life

We all have a relationship with our emotions. That may sound weird, but we have a relationship with our emotions like we can have a relationship with our partner. In what way, then? An emotion isn't a thing or person, is it? I will explain.

A happiness seeker often has a bad relationship with his negative emotions, because these stand in the way of the feeling of happiness. The consequences of this are great, for emotions that are not allowed to exist become the centre of our attention. And instead of us getting powered by our feelings, our negative emotions seize power. You will discover that suppressing unpleasant feelings brings about the opposite of what we want and that emotions are not made at all to be suppressed. In this chapter, I will discuss that we can learn from emotions, including the negative ones. Perfectionism and a taboo on failure boost negative emotions, and, as mentioned in the previous chapter, 'perfection' and 'avoiding fear' are two elements of our manner of thinking about happiness. Because a negative relationship with emotions stands in the way of sustainable happiness, I teach you how to get started with accepting nasty emotions.

'If we had only positive emotions, then our species would have become extinct long ago.'

Martin Seligman

The taboo on negative emotions

What do most people do when they experience an unpleasant emotion? Right, they try to get rid of them, push them away or ignore them. Our happiness mindset does not allow negative emotions and makes them even taboo. But in that way, we create a bigger problem than the original emotion itself. A suppressed emotion hasn't disappeared: it has been suppressed.

Emotions are important experiences for people and I am amazed time and time again how confused our relations with emotions can be. In the pursuit of happiness, not only being happy has tremendous value, but also the associated emotions such as joy, contentment and euphoria stand out head and shoulders above the other, often less fun, emotions. It goes without saying that if happiness is high on the rating scale, joy is an important feeling. The overvaluation of the one puts the other emotions (fear, sadness, anger) in a very bad light. Men don't cry, anger is taboo, and fear is the opposite of success. Some people indeed go so far that they really hate their nasty emotions with all the associated distorted consequences.

> 'But feelings cannot be ignored,
> however unreasonable or
> ungrateful they may seem.'
>
> *Anne Frank*

Emotions have to move!

Hardly anybody realizes that the word emotion stems from the Latin word 'emovere' which amounts to 'move', 'move outwards'. Moving outwards is exactly what people are trying to prevent with their taboo emotions. Because a negative emotion does not fit in the being-happy image and seems to be fully at variance with the recommended happiness strategies, the average person believes that permitting negative emotions will entail catastrophic consequences. You see, negative emotions might take us over. Just imagine: If I should start crying over something I'm genuinely sad about, those tears might go on forever and condemn me to a life full of tears and stigma.

No, then rather the lid on it, because once I release the beast, my negative feelings, the beast has me in its power. The remedy for dealing with those 'enormously dangerous' feelings is to combat and overcome them. We should fight our emotions, which means that we implicitly give ourselves the message that our emotions are not good. The fight with our desires and the concept of living in sin, such as described in the Bible, are examples of that. In the past, it was obviously not understood so well that we experience emotions when doing something meaningful. It was apparently also unknown that by suppressing the emotions you also suppress meaning, and that this, in the long run, will cause you to feel nothing anymore. 'I have no feeling about that', said the man who had just divorced from the love of his life.

Yes, unpleasant emotions are tricky, because you need to do some soul searching and ask yourself if your conclusions are correct, if the emotion you are experiencing has something to do with what is actually happening. You see, it is fairly simple to experience emotions purely through your personal interpretation of an event. If you allow your feelings to move you have to face your interpretations and, moreover, to develop a healthier relationship with yourself. By fighting and resisting emotions, you will simply not get to know the intention of your feelings. Shutting a feeling out causes that feeling to remain in the background, with the result that it has you in its clutches, and that is the very thing you are trying to prevent. It also ensures that you don't get to know the meaning of your own emotions. Moving, however unpopular, is the road to a healthier relationship with yourself. The example below of my conversation with Gerard illustrates how opposing a feeling does not change feelings.

GERARD

Gerard has come to me in a roundabout way and tells me he has been down for a long time. After some explanation of his situation, he tells me that he always feels so tense.

'In the morning I get up with it, then it starts already', Gerard says.

'What starts then?'

'That tension in my body, in my neck and my breathing. I have had this for many years, you know.'

'What are you doing with it?'

'What do you mean, I get a bit seized by panic and when the tension persists, I'm just at a loss what to do.'

'What's so bad about that tension then?'

'Then I get crying spells, I just do not know how to handle them.'

'How do you react then to this tension?'

'Well, I have taught myself to suppress this tension.'

'Why?'

'Because my whole family is troubled by my crying spells and I don't want to do that to them.'

'Have you ever tried to accept your tension instead of fighting it?'

'Please, I'm not here for that, I'm looking for something to suppress it.'

'How effective has this approach been to date?'

'Er, not really.'

Because Gerard does not know what to do with his tension, he stays in combat with it. And although he has been dealing a long time in this way with his uncomfortable feelings, he has not succeeded in suppressing the tension with all the nasty feelings that come with it. Looked at it this way, you can say that his tension has him in its power instead of the other way round. Due to the fight, he doesn't get to know the meaning of his feelings and therefore does not learn to respond adequately to them.

The lessons of negative emotions

Emotions help us in two ways: firstly, they help us to dwell on what might be important for us, and secondly, they give us insight into whether our interpretation of events shouldn't be updated in order to get a more accurate perspective of reality.

Thus, grief teaches you to have an eye for the value of a loss. Your heart becomes softer and it becomes clearer to you what is valuable for you in your life. This way you may be able to replace what you've lost or to keep close to you what you're likely to lose. Anger gives you information about how your values have been encroached on and helps you to stand up for yourself and defend your values when necessary. Fear is very important because it gives you insight into what could be dangerous in your life and a threat to your values. Obviously, you can also experience all these emotions when there is no actual danger, infringement of your values, or loss. Then the emotion gives you insight into the fact that something is not right in your interpretation of reality. Anyhow, if you overrate your joy, your ability to embrace the other emotions will diminish.

'Intolerance is a bad embracer.'

So, in order to become an emotionally intelligent being who can choose whether to tuck something away or to admit it, you need all your emotions! Yes indeed, we need them all, the negative and the positive ones. For without all the emotions at our disposal, we simply cannot respond effectively to the challenges that life has in store for us.

Developing the ability to embrace the negative emotions, just like you welcome the joyful, helps you to cope much more effectively with awkward life experiences.

Rather paradoxically, tolerance for all your emotions helps you not to get stuck in your experience. In every relationship, every work project, every family situation and many other situations, setbacks and obstructions can

occur. The ability to embrace the negative emotions that arise then, causes the emotions to lose their power. It is precisely the fear of the negative emotions that makes the emotion powerful. Think of the following scenario: Suppose you are requested to push a kangaroo ball under water and to keep it there, how big is the chance that you will succeed? Right, not so great. Now, replace the kangaroo ball with an emotion that you don't like about yourself, such as uncertainty or a fear you have or grief you don't want to be reminded of. Imagine that you try to suppress this emotion just like the kangaroo ball. Will you succeed? No, of course not, indeed, the suppression of a negative emotion leads to the emotion really keeping you in its power. For fighting against something that apparently cannot be suppressed will ultimately give it the power to control you.

Perfect fear of failure

Failure is tricky in creating the perfect world. Failure does not fit completely in that picture, or actually not at all.

Failure is often an even greater taboo than a nasty emotion in the pursuit of the ideal happiness experience. To keep annoying emotions under one's thumb, one has to be especially averse to failure and has to strive for perfection. Failure and having a criterion have a lot to do with each other. You can really only fail if your criterion is just a little stricter than your ability to meet that criterion. Now, the person with anxiety has an often miraculous 'solution' for the failure problem. You go for perfection! You make the yardstick so exceptionally severe that you are sure you cannot meet it and then let yourself have it.

PITCHING INTO YOURSELF
I often come across examples of not accepting annoying feelings, even on the tennis court.
'Twerp!' I hear my tennis buddy say to himself when he manages to hit the ball over the fence after five very long warm-up minutes. Unbelievable. He expects to be so warmed up in five minutes that his body can do perfectly what he has in mind, apart from the fact that he, just like me, is a normal mediocre player. I ask him: 'What, by the way, is the purpose of slashing at yourself like this?' 'To get better', he says resolutely. 'Does it work?', I ask him casually. 'No, it doesn't', he shouts even more pissed off than before. 'Why, then, do you treat yourself like this', I ask him. Apparently, it's getting too personal. He indicates that he would like to go on playing.

'Perfectionism is an ultimate expression of a fear-driven endeavour to prevent failure in any way whatsoever.'

Oliver Burkeman

Problematic rituals

The happiness seeker who is intolerant of his or her own failure often follows the following track. You have very high expectations of yourself that do not work out, after which a swearing ritual begins (I must be better, I need a kick under my butt, what a pathetic case I am), or a shame ritual (if only no-one has seen this, I'm just going to work harder), a guilt ritual (I must make up for it, no matter what it is, I have to make up for it), a fear ritual (I'm not going to do anything anymore, or I'm going to panic because I can't do this anyway) or a grief ritual (I'm not good enough, no one likes me).

If you can't tolerate your own feelings, you'll end up getting farther away from your goals. The big problem of perfectionists is that they usually try to find a solution for their problem within perfectionist frameworks. They are the enormously hard workers in my coaching, people who are really doing their best and even work overtime for it. Besides, every boss wants to employ someone like that, because they work flat out. Unfortunately, they often end up at home with burnout or severe strain. What first seemed like a good investment for the boss suddenly becomes quite a debit entry... Yes, if you always try to find solutions within the same frameworks, you will always arrive at the same point.

> ## 'If you do what you always did, you get what you always got.'
> *Albert Einstein*

Giving negative emotions a place

In the *ZEST FOR LIFE* part, I go more deeply into how you can give negative emotions a place and even embrace them. The exercise below is for people who still need to get used to the idea that emotions are good for you...

Try this technique that I developed a few years ago for perfectionists who are averse to therapy or coaching, but thirst after change.

The F... It! technique

Into what ritual do you lapse when you fail? Are you going to swear, are you ashamed, do you feel guilty, anxious or sad?

→ Think of something you accept. Then say aloud 'F**k it!' (in the sense of 'doesn't matter'). Feel strongly for a moment that you believe this. Feel the 'F**ck it' completely, 'Oh well, what does it matter.' Practice this a few times just so long until you feel that 'it doesn't matter'.

→ If one day you utterly fail, say just before you slip back into your ritual: 'F**ck it, what does it really matter after all.' Repeat this as often as necessary until you get a smile on your face.

Summary

To be really happy, emotions must move. Suppressing feelings creates more unhappiness than letting annoying feelings move. Fear of failure and the urge for perfection are excellent motives to suppress awkward emotions. Fear of failure, craving for perfection and being averse to annoying emotions are eminently happiness deeds in the hope that no negativity will manifest in your life... However, it is exactly the resistance to the negative which strengthens that negative. In this way, negative emotions are paradoxically given power over us. The lessons we can learn from our emotions are:

→ Emotions must move because then the emotion no longer has you, but you have the emotion.

→ You can't be happy if you don't embrace all your emotions, for negative emotions cannot be suppressed, in the end, they don't go away as a result.

→ Emotions teach you something about what you think is important. You get important information about what you find meaningful by experiencing your emotion.

→ Emotions give you information whether you need to look more accurately at reality. Your emotions teach you whether your interpretation of events matches reality. For example, if someone with a knife stands in front of you, it makes sense to feel fear, but if you feel fear when thinking of a spider that isn't present, then that fear is trying to inform you of the mistake you made. It's time for an emotion update.

→ You can't be happy if you're intolerant of your own failure. The taboo on failure ultimately strengthens your chance to fail. Hence if you think like a perfectionist, you will have to be on an infinite journey to perfection, because one thing is certain: perfection can hardly ever be achieved.

→ Perfectionism is the ultimate expression of your fear of failure.

We have now looked at happiness on a social and emotional level. In the next chapter, it becomes clear that language usage and happiness are closely intertwined. Words are symbols for meaning. Happiness is much talked about, but what is the real meaning of happiness? In the next chapter, I explain how the way we formulate happiness affects the way we think about happiness.

3.
The language of Happiness

Our usage of language and our experience of happiness are closely intertwined. The language we use is a reflection of deeper emotional processes. Using language, we express on the surface what we experience deep inside. Unfortunately, the journey from inside to outside is often blurred to such an extent that what comes out of our mouth often does not correspond to what we really mean. From feeling to words can be a considerable undertaking. Conveying your experience in such a way that the words you use effectively describe your inner perception, proves to be tricky for most of us. In our language there are pitfalls. It may seem that we put into words what we mean, but if you listen carefully, you discover that the words you use create a misleading veil. The problem is getting still bigger because we don't realize that we organize our lives on the basis of descriptions that are misleading. In this chapter, you will get acquainted with the way language influences your actions, and I end the chapter with tips and exercises to discover how you can become more specific. This way you get more insight into what happiness and dejection mean to you.

Superficial conversations

Who doesn't simply want to be happy? But if it is so difficult to achieve, how everyday is it then, after all? One would expect to think that everything that is usual should truly be very ordinary, effortless, obvious? Ordinary happiness is evidently much more unusual than people realize and since our brains, seen from an evolutionary viewpoint, have been constructed for opportunism, we are talking about it as if it were the commonest thing in the world.[8]

Imagine that you were to say, 'I just want to drink water.' What is happening then inside you? In the average person, something matter-of-course arises, a sense of readiness to take action, initiative. Water, you see, is a very specific subject, clearly defined, with a clear purpose and a very clear *internal representation*. A glass of water is something you can see in front of you and can grasp in your mind. It satisfies the underlying desire to drink water. Linguistically you would say that your internal perception (also called internal representation) corresponds to what you express in words and behaviour (also called the surface structure of an experience). Often, this relationship between the language we speak and the internal representation it refers to is out the window. With all its consequences: miscommunication, relationship problems, lack of clarity about the turn you want to take in your life et cetera.

'The desire to live a happy life is one of the biggest problems you can saddle yourself with.'

Although the desire for a happy life is a valid wish in our society, there is something very specific going on when we put 'happy life' under a linguistic magnifying glass. And since our language usage is a reflection of deeper processes, language analysis is relevant.

From a linguistic point of view, you can say that the desire for a happy life is one of the biggest problems you can saddle yourself with. That's pretty easy to explain.

---

8   In Chapter 5 I delve deeper into the importance of this statement (I just want to be happy) in the emergence of depressive feelings.

First, it is one of the greatest wishes you can utter. A happy life, it's quite a bit. How much would indeed need to change to get all the elements of a happy life done? From health, to finance, from children to career, from family to personal needs and spiritual desires... our happiness is rather swayed. Second, no one knows (and you probably don't either) what you are referring to when you refer to a happy life. It is so nonspecific that you have or get no grip on what this means. The combination of these two factors ensures that you have formulated an (unconsciously) unattainable goal for yourself. Unachievable goals usually make you give up and get frustrated.

The intention of 'happiness'

You could say that 'just wanting to be happy' is simply poorly worded. There is a great danger if you do not take a critical look at this statement. Which? That you just keep chasing after your 'just-wanting-to be-happy' idea, whereas it actually is only a description of a superficial need. It is only the beginning of a wish, a grand unspecific desire. The vagueness creates a desire, but a desire for what? It seems so obvious, but it is actually nothing...

This process of deception is a very normal process in people. Do you know the feeling that sometimes it can take hours or days before you can put into words what you actually experience? 'This is it, this is what it is about.' People very often don't say what they mean.

SAD

Recently I told a friend that it didn't make me very happy that she was so hard to reach. I found this difficult because I wanted to discuss some important issues with her. I hadn't so much as finished when her reaction was: 'So what can you do to reach me for certain?' and 'I also feel a bit pushed because I have the feeling that you want me to do something' and 'Why do you do make such a fuss about it?'

*The conversation continued like this for a while and I didn't
have the idea that she had heard what I said, until she stopped
after ten minutes or so to talk to me and suddenly said:
'It makes me sad.' For the first time in the conversation, she
said something about her own deeper experience in connection
with my remark. Until then she had only responded and tried
to convince me that I had to adapt my wishes. After quite a
bit of rambling, she came to her inner experience when I said,
'It doesn't make me very happy that I cannot reach you'. She
said: 'It makes me sad because I like to be there for you when
you want to discuss something important, I have the feeling
that I fail while what I want more than anything is to be there
for you too.' That was the first moment in the conversation that
changed the tone of the conversation, and that we both became
softer and opener to each other.*

In our daily communication, we often react before we
know what is being referred to. This can cause feelings of
misunderstanding and even quarrel. When we can find
each other in our deeper intentions we can experience
instant connection. And that is one of our deepest wishes.

Misleading usage of language

Happiness is a noun, and an important feature of
nouns is that they don't denote action. According
to transformational grammar, 'happiness' is a
nominalization[9]. Politicians use a great many
nominalizations in their statements. Think of words like
potential, prosperity, values and norms, modernization,
education, innovation, Europe, advance and so on.

Nominalisations obscure messages because they give
the suggestion that these statements refer to something
concrete or some action while this is not the case. Thus,
the listener gets the feeling that something of significance
is being said while this is not really so. And because
these statements are meaningless, the recipients of the

9   https://en.wikipedia.org/wiki/Transformational_grammar

statements (meaning 'we') have got to attach meaning to them ourselves. And since we all have a different background, other experiences, beliefs and meanings, chances are that what I think up (and of course know for certain) about what the statement means will be different from the meaning my neighbour attributes to it. How many business initiatives haven't gone to pieces based on this? Or how many relationships haven't come in rough weather due to the assumption that you knew what the other meant, but that eventually, the expectations you had of being together turned out to be totally different...

HAVING A GRIP ON THINGS

My friend Lex wants to tell his story and asks if I would like to have a beer with him. He is a bit under the weather and after a long speech he says:

'Yes man, I just want to be happy, like everyone else.' Because I had no inkling of what he was talking about I asked him:

'In what way would you just like to be happy?'

'Well, I just want things to come more naturally, I'm struggling all the time, see?'

'Well, no, not exactly.'

'I'm struggling with my relationship, family, money and you name it.'

'Jeez, man, then you're pretty down-and-out. If on all these fronts everything under the sun is going on, how can you possibly be happy?'

'I just want to have a grip on my life.'

'How exactly do you want to have a grip on your life?'

'I would like to have the feeling that I have my life under control again.'

'Under control?'

'Yes, that I am back at the helm, I'm having my life lived for me so much.'

'Ah, you want to be at the helm...'

By continuing to ask for the action behind Lex' statements, slowly but surely it becomes clearer what he means by 'just want to be happy'. The vague state of 'being happy'

*becomes again palpable for him by recovering the missing
activity in his statements. This is fun for me because I
understand Lex better now, but it is even much more fun for
Lex because he now knows what he is looking for and might
work on.*

In other words, 'just want to be happy' is too vague. We
seem to be saying something, but don't really know what
we are referring to. But also in statements such as: 'He is
a bully', 'She wants recognition', 'I need to improve my
communication' it is not clear what is really meant. For
example, 'Improve your communication'. What exactly?
Should I talk louder or softer? Articulate better? Write
flawlessly? Asking more thoroughly or listen better? The
possibilities are endless. In these statements the underlying
activity is described in the form of a noun. The action
has become a thing. Your thoughts get paralyzed and
you are not looking further for the actual purpose of the
utterance.

'What people come for is seldom what it is about.'

These linguistic confusions we also create in ourselves by
embracing the vagueness of our own statements as the
truth. We go and act on the basis of this mental deception,
which means that we are moving in a direction that is
not really the direction that is essential for us. Indeed,
the search for happiness can keep us pretty busy. This
may mean that for many years you are busy wanting to
be just happy, but are unable to accomplish it because it's
not clear what you're looking for, while you nevertheless
assume that you know what you're looking for. Confusing?
Yes, that's exactly what it is. We can send ourselves on a
journey in the full belief that we are on the right track,
without ever arriving at the destination. And then, on top

of everything, we are even disappointed with it. Our use of language can be quite misleading.[10]

Tips
What can you do to formulate a more accurate pursuit of happiness?

❶ Learn to become more specific: Happier with what exactly? Your job? Relationship? Perspective on life?

❷ Formulate that which you have an influence on: Your experience of happiness is strongly related to the feeling that you can change or influence something. Being happy has a lot to do with your sense of influence. If you are not happy with your hairstyle, you can go to the hairdresser's and do something about your appearance. If you are not happy with your relationship and you are stuck to a mortgage then you may feel that you cannot influence your happiness situation. In that sense, your experience of happiness is directly linked to your sense of influence on your life and your situation. Please, formulate what you can influence.

❸ Formulate what is important to you: there are few things in people that are exactly the same as in other people, which makes you want to learn to clarify what you are referring to. It is not for nothing that one person can be happy in a hut on the beach and the next one must absolutely have a bath to feel happy and glad.

❹ Formulate what you want to change: being happy is time-bound. Knowing that something is going to change is a completely different experience from having the idea that this will be so forever. For example, if your energy level is low at the moment, please describe that in the months to come you want to have more energy. For example, if you feel lonely, please describe what you want to change. You can start with the words: 'What I want to change is...' Then compare your current situation with what you long for and become aware of what needs to change to get from A to B.

❺ Formulate with the right comparison in mind: our happiness experience is linked to recent experiences. If your previous relationship was even worse than this one, you will feel relatively

10 For a detailed description of the meta-model as used in Neuro Linguistic Programming: Https://nl.wikipedia. Org/wiki/Meta model.

happier because you know it can be even worse. If you refer to that goddess who you came across on holiday, that girl you were in love with head over heels and this memory has shaped your image of what an ideal relationship adds up to, then, with your kids on your lap and your wife badgering about money and whatever you do isn't good anyway, you can sometimes feel pretty unhappy.

Be more specific

If you want to know more about your being-happy wishes, please take the time to answer the following questions:

→ Which thoughts make me happy? What should I keep in mind to experience happiness? What kind of thoughts make me happy

→ What kind of feelings should I experience? What do I need to feel to experience happiness?

→ What should I do and what actions should I take to make me feel happy?

→ To be happy, what kind of relationships should I build?

→ To be happy, what outcomes should I experience?

Define the cause-effect relationships

It is useful to have more clarity about what caused your feelings of happiness and misery. The relationship between cause and effect is one you may be able to influence.

Just think about how your current feelings have arisen. You have not become dissatisfied, dejected or sorrowful just like that. Ask yourself:

1. What happiness relationships are you talking about?? What exactly are your feelings of happiness and misery about?

Which relationship(s) do you want to improve?

What relationship do you have with adversity?

What relationship do you have with intimacy?

What relationship do you have with being successful?

What relationship do you have with failure?

What relationship do you have with negative emotions?

What relationship do you have to your career?

What relationship do you have with your friends and family?

What relationship do you have with spirituality?

2. What is the relationship between your lifestyle and your experience of happiness?

3. What matters influence your experience of happiness?

4. What is the cause of my being unhappy?

Summary

Our language usage hinders a happy life. Being happy is too great a wish, perhaps the greatest. It is also a nonspecific wish which makes being happy unachievable (and for a dejected person even despondently unachievable). Language creates action, but if we do not have a clear picture of what we actually mean, it will create the wrong action. You could say that 'just being happy' is really just badly formulated. That is why we are going to re-define *happiness* in the next chapter.

4.
Being lucky

Language has a greater impact on our daily lives and unconscious experience than we think at first. You saw that in the previous chapter. Giving meaning to something helps us to be able to define something, and, once we can define it, we know how to deal with it. We all know the definitions of happiness to a certain extent, but do we know what it means to be happy? I have found that happiness has several definitions and that we are chasing the wrong definition. There are two definitions of happiness and the most widely used is our biggest happiness enemy. *Being lucky* is rarely associated with being happy or dejection, it seems to have little to do with it. Yet there are essential indications in this interpretation of happiness that will give us new insights into the dejected person's perception of the world and that can help us seek solutions for lasting happiness in our lives.

Going after happiness leads to depression

I believe that with our pursuit of happiness we are on a wrong track. I can reasonably substantiate this on the strength of the thousands of clients I have had occasion to coach. We are even on a dangerous track. One of the dangers lies in something very fundamental: If you do not know what you are aiming for, you may find yourself in the wrong place. It has already become clear that 'being happy' as a great elusive goal paralyzes our brain, but there is still something much subtler going on.

We make assumptions. We assume that we know how things work and what the meaning of things in our lives is.

But, more often than you think, our assumptions appear to be ideas that we have not fully thought out. Adopted from parents, examples, boyfriends and girlfriends, and of course from the media as well. We are constantly told what happiness is supposed to be, what it looks like, what its scents, tastes, sounds and feelings are. Day in and day out this is subtly presented to us and depending on what sub-group you belong to, happiness has its own unique meaning and ambition.

I think that our pursuit of happiness even has a very serious effect. Our pursuit of happiness leads in a large group of people to chronic gloom, disappointment, relationships that fail time and again, chronic searching and even depression.

I recognize that it gives you a fright. While all this time you have been thinking that you are doing well, you are told offhand that searching for happiness may have made you unhappy. I had that too, but it didn't only give me a fright, a lot of things fell in place. In my conversation with John (see the introduction) I got that insight. All of a sudden I realized that the constant pursuit of prettier, better, more fun and happier had created a huge problem. An unintentional by-product of a striving for our extraordinary capabilities. It felt as if the world was upside down. Some of the things I aspired to and firmly believed in in my life, hoping that my life would become even more enjoyable, ultimately made me more unfortunate than I could hold possible. I did my best to stick to various success formulas like the seven steps to this... and the seven steps to that... and also had professionally applied myself completely to the research into successful strategies. I could honestly say that people can do a lot more than we think possible, but suddenly I understood that our wish for happiness has a dark shadow side. And all of my body told me this was right.

Our aspiring to happiness has become our happiness enemy because we clutch at every happiness straw and put it in the centre of our attention, in order not to be confronted with rejection, failure and annoying emotions. Just think about being happy and all the related matters like being successful, effective and having turned out well. Just think about everything we have been brought up on based on our survival mechanism and our fear-drivenness. We have gone to chase after something so unspecific that we can never reach that destination... But does this mean that we cannot experience happiness in our lives? No, certainly not! To be able to experience lasting happiness in our lives, we need to define more specifically what happiness actually is. You have to recognize when you're *lucky*.

Two kinds of happiness

If you have a good think about it, there are two ways of being in good spirits: being happy and being lucky. The first describes a kind of state, a mood and the second an experience. Let's call them 'happiness 1' and 'happiness 2' for the sake of convenience.

HAPPINESS 1

Being happy can be defined as being satisfied with the current living conditions or with life as it is now presenting itself to you. Happiness is associated here with feelings of joy, harmony and satisfaction. Seen in this way happiness is: 'The experience of joy, contentment, or positive well-being, combined with a sense that one's life is good, meaningful, and worthwhile.'[11] Or, to take the average of some dictionary definitions: 'Happiness is a pleasant state of contentment.'

11 Sonja Lyubomirsky, *The how of happiness*, 2007

The interesting thing about all these descriptions is that they describe a kind of end states[12]. A chain of nouns describing states of mind or moods. Only nobody tells you what exactly this means and how you could get there. It creates a feeling of 'if only had this'. A desire without travel book, something others also have and what you and I would also like to have. It's almost a magical state that you can conjure up in your life 'with a daub of pink here and a daub of pink there.'

This definition of happiness and being happy is vague and unspecific. In fact, this description describes a kind of ideal state of mind that is not linked to any specific endeavour. It is, as it were, a state you are in, a kind of emotion that you have. This kind of happiness and being happy is the kind the average person refers to at a get-together, in good conversations with loved ones and in therapy or coaching sessions.

HAPPINESS 2

The second definition of happiness, being lucky, is of a different kind. There is more activity in it, it says something about the future, and instead of how your state should be, it creates a state. Being lucky is more tangible and so lives more up to the goal of happiness. Being lucky is a definition of happiness that we all know but is rarely linked to being happy. This should be done, in my opinion, especially if you understand the depressive mindset better.

Happiness, in the sense of being lucky, means to have been favoured by an unforeseen event. In that sense, happiness means the prosperity that falls to a person (without their

---

12 Your state is the sum of your mental, emotional and physical activity in one particular moment. Your state tremendously influences how you interpret your experiences and your outlook on the world. Thus, a state is more than a state of mind because a state of mind chiefly describes a person's emotional state. For convenience's sake I use in *Happiness is Depressing* the words state of mind as synonymous with state.

being able to control it). Being lucky refers to prosperous, favourable and blessed. So, if you want to be happy, you really want that things will thrive in your life. That your undertaking is favourably disposed to you and you are blessed in the journey you are setting out on. Notice how that influences your thinking and state. Experience for a moment how it feels to focus on prosperity. A great state if you let it come in.

Happiness in this sense of the word has traditionally been associated with four important qualities: light, fate, coincidence and prosperity. These qualities are important in the emergence of depression, in finding light in that darkness and thus also in experiencing more happiness in your life.

1. Light
Being lucky is originally linked to light, like for example 'seeing the light'. This is a very interesting relationship, for, as will come up in the following chapters, it's exactly 'light' which is a crucial element in the development and continuing existence of the depressive mindset and thus dejection.

2. Fate - What you have decided - Your destination
Having good luck does not quite seem to happen to us, after all. It says something about how we experience our fate and therefore what your destiny is. This is again a fascinating reference because happiness is evidently not a passive state you receive. It's more of an active act, which says something about how you can deal with your fate and find your destiny. In the following chapters you will discover how fate, deciding and your destiny are essential elements to transform the dejected mindset.

3. Coincidence
This is actually the simplest definition of luck, and although that may be difficult to grasp now, bad luck plays an important role in the development of dejection. And, as you will discover later in one of the techniques

to experience more happiness in your life, coincidence plays a very special role in our daily happiness experience. Seamlessly linked up with this:

4. Prosperity - Advantage - What turns out well - Succeeding - Faith in a positive result
This says something about the future and a confidence in that future. On a deeper level these definitions evoke a sense of self-assurance. And here too we get a crucial clue about the relationship between the emergence of depression and that possibility to open the door to more happiness. The combination of coincidence and 'that it succeeds' proves to be a very powerful builder of happiness.

Feeling the difference
Now say instead of 'I just want to be happy' aloud 'I want my relationship to prosper', 'I want my career to prosper', 'I want my life to prosper'. What's the difference?

Summary
After we have seen how our ideas about happiness are on a cultural, emotional and linguistic level, we know that we have to view happiness in a different way. It so happens that we have collectively adopted the being-happy definition and made it a guiding feature in our pursuit of happiness. We all strive for that pleasant state of satisfaction. Spend heaps of money to experience that state, and in our stubbornness, we continue to look for this unattainable utopia.

But our going for happiness makes us dejected. Happiness enemy number one is our definition of happiness, so we have to redefine happiness before we can work at a happier existence. It is extraordinary to realize that the new definition of happiness in the form of 'prosperity' and 'blessed' gives important clues for a happier existence. But above all, that it yields insights that help to understand dejection better.

Just being happy becomes a lot more common when we seek a happiness which puts us in motion, offers hope and creates light in the darkness. Being lucky gives us a much clearer picture of happiness in our lives, a much more active state and the expectation of prosperity. In the following parts, it will become clearer why the redefinition of happiness is so important for solving dejection, and how the elements of being lucky contribute so significantly to the transformation of low-spiritedness. The new perspectives on depression that I have found paint a new picture of what a depressed person experiences. The new approach that makes this possible can be read in part 3 *ZEST FOR LIFE*, but first we explore the inner landscape of dejection. Why? If you don't understand where you are, then you don't know either how to attain where you want to be.

Introduction part 2
Depression

Do you ever feel down, gloomy or don't you know for sure what's the matter with you? Aren't you feeling as happy as you would like to be, dissatisfied? Would you, too, like to be happy as described in the previous chapter? The weird thing with depressive feelings is that people who have them just haven't been feeling quite happy for a long-time but don't link that feeling to low spirits. It is obviously important to make a distinction between the medical diagnosis of depression and feeling depressed.

> 'I'm doing better since it's OK that sometimes I'm doing not so well.'
>
> *Unknown*

Gloomy people often feel alone, but if you feel gloomy, you're not alone: 'More than a million Dutch suffered from depression in 2014' headlined the Central Agency for Statistics on January 25, 2016. A staggering figure that amounts to eight percent of the population! That same day this was nuanced somewhat, because the Trimbos Institute lowered this percentage down to 5.2 percent, of which only two percent go to the GP. Most people obviously don't. An important nuance in this research is that the Trimbos Institute uses the official depression questionnaire of the World Health Organization (WHO), which is based on the official diagnosis as described in the *DSM (Diagnostic and Statistical Manual of Mental Disorders)*, the internationally used handbook for psychiatric diseases. On the other hand, the CBS only asked how people were feeling, to which the answer 'depressed' was given. Medical editor Wim Köhler of Dutch newspaper NRC pertinently raises the question: 'But what is depression really, if the figures can be so different?[13]

> 'In Western society we
> have developed an ethics
> of happiness, deviations
> from it are seen as an
> indication of sickness.'
>
> *Professor Christopher Dowrick*

The difference between what people experience and the medical diagnosis of depression is an interesting difference. It touches on a subject that is little talked about: what do we really know about depression and how have our ideas about depression come into being? As will appear in the following chapters, much isn't clear about depression while people are talking about it as if everything were already clear. According to the DSM, depression is a disease, but that answer isn't satisfactory. The generally accepted assumptions about what depression is, and how it arises, cause medications to be prescribed more and more often. This approach stands in the way of a structural solution for gloominess. In this section I will show you what restrictions our assumptions cause in how depression is generally thought of. While doing so, I take a critical look at the medical view on depression. Moreover, I map how depression arises and what the main causes of dejection are.

Instead of considering depression as a disease that has simply arisen, I look at depression for what it is: a symptom complex. I don't research depression from the outside, but I view dejection from the perspective of the depressive person. I give answers to questions like: 'What does a dejected person experience?' and 'What does the inner

13 Wim Köhler, NRC.checkt, Wednesday 28 January 2016

world of a depressed person look like?' This inner world could be seen as a landscape. In this depressive landscape you can discover surprising connecting points about the genesis and transformation of dejection. In the last chapter of this part I am zooming in on the relationship between happiness and dejection. I show how our pursuit of happiness makes for dejection and how the depressive landscape gives us insight into how we can experience more happiness in our lives. In the part that follows, *ZEST FOR LIFE* you will be taken to a new world via the depressive landscape, step by step. In this way, you discover what depression actually is. Don't worry, because when your inner world becomes visible to you, it also becomes clear what needs to be done to be happy again. Every exercise that is described in *ZEST FOR LIFE* ensures that, slowly but surely, more and more light is going to shine in the dark and that a landscape full of zest for life becomes visible to you.

5.
Just not happy

According to statistics there is a depression epidemic going on because, as will be apparent, depression is nothing but growing worldwide. It is not for nothing that depression is called the new flu. That there is a relationship between the degree of happiness we experience and depression is not new. That we can learn from depression what happiness is for us, and how we might become happy, that, indeed, is new. About depression very much is already known and in this chapter, I mention the facts and symptoms of depression.

Gloom and happiness

What does happiness have to do with depression and vice versa? Maybe it's an open door, but depressed people are not the most joyful people. They are often sad, have had enough of it, are in a sombre mood and find less meaning in life than the average happy person.

If you were to write down two extremes, then super happy is the one and suicidal the other end. One wants to celebrate life and the other to end life. One finds meaning in seemingly trivial things and the other finds no significance in the weightiest matters. Actually happiness and depression have a lot to do with each other. They are a kind of opposites of each other you could say, but again not quite...

By and large, depressed people have not been depressed throughout their lives and they have still somehow ended up in it one way or another. How does a normal person end up in depression? What can you learn from the mindset of a depressed person about how happiness can come into our lives? And how could you 'de-gloom' a gloomy mindset again? The answers to these questions will give you a new outlook on gloom and happiness in your life.

Depression occurs in varying degrees: light, moderate and severe. The ideas in this book apply to all categories, but certain types of depressive complaints are ignored and anyone walking around with suicidal thoughts is advised to look for a specialist.[14]

Facts about Depression

Ask any gloomy person what he or she wants and the usual 'nothing', 'don't care', 'don't feel like it' and 'fuck off', often is followed by 'I just want to be happy'. The first problem with that statement 'to be happy' has extensively been discussed in Part 1 *HAPPINESS*, the 'just' (or 'simply') I would like to discuss for a moment. If it were as simple as suggested, the person would be able to switch easily from one state of mind to another. However, it's not that simple. Why, actually? Why isn't it normal for people and not normal at all for a depressed person to be happy? It is difficult to get a grip on our dark states of mind and vague feelings. You can be stuck in them for weeks, months, even years. Some never get it (completely) on track.

To answer these questions, I first put some facts about depression in a row. After that I will, in the following chapters, have a critical look at the subjects below:

1. The assumptions about depression and the *DSM kind of thinking*;
2. How depression arises;
3. What depression actually is;

14 Depression coupled with bipolar problems, psychosis and demonstrable genetic or medical causes are left aside.

4. What is happening in the mind of a (chronically) depressed person;
5. What exactly the relationship is between happiness and depression.

The WHO (World Health Organization) calls depression the hidden burden. Hidden because depression is taboo for most people, it isn't talked about and therefore isn't treated. Three hundred and fifty million people worldwide suffer from some form of depression and it is thus the main cause of human suffering in the world.[15] Not only the individuals themselves suffer from this chronic form of gloom but also the people around them.

Persistent gloom, little energy and difficulty with daily functioning are some general symptoms. Depression often gives such a stigma that people don't talk about it; depression is a taboo. Depression often begins at an early age and more women than men suffer from it worldwide. Young depressed mothers often can't take proper care of their children with all that entails. Each year, a million people who suffer from depression commit suicide and for every person who succeeds in doing so, twenty people make an attempt. This means that 20 million people a year suffer so much or think they are bothering others so much that they think they themselves and their environment are better off if they are no longer there.[16]

According to experts, the disease depression must be given a global health priority. In a study published in PLOS Medicine in 2013, two hundred other diseases and accidents that cause severe suffering in daily functioning were compared to depression. Depression comes second in the list of most debilitating disorders compared to the other diseases. And worldwide only a fraction of the people who need it are given the proper counselling.

---

15 Helen Briggs, *Depression: 'second biggest cause of disability' in the world*, BBC News, 6 november 2013
16 WHO Depression fact sheet – www.who.int/mental_health

Antidepressants as appeasement

Following the sudden death of actor Robin Williams in August 2014, depression and suicide hit the headlines. Research by the English Royal College of Psychiatry has shown that less than one third of the people with the most common mental health problems (depression, anxiety, ADHD) are treated for these problems. Professor Simon Wessely, president of the College, says: 'If these were the figures of the treatment of cancer patients, no one would tolerate this.' Most people with mental or emotional problems in the United Kingdom have to wait eighteen weeks to two years for some counselling. A consequence of this is a huge increase in the prescription of antidepressants because there is simply no money for other and deeper counselling, such as the so-called talk therapies. Although these are ultimately cheaper and better than medicines, the National Health Service system (similar to health insurance companies) does not provide money for the guidance of this increasingly larger group in society.[17]

17 Sarah Boseley, *Two-thirds of Britons with depression get no treatment*, The Guardian, 13 augustus 2014

The nine symptoms

The nine symptoms of a depressive disorder according to the DSM-V are:

1. Dejection for almost the whole day, almost every day. You can experience it like this yourself or others notice it. In young people it often manifests itself in irritability.
2. You clearly have diminished interest and fun in almost all activities throughout most of the day, almost every day.
3. You lose weight or become overweight without wanting to; this is accompanied by a decrease or increase in your appetite.
4. You have sleep complaints: you can't sleep or you're sleeping far too much.
5. You feel agitated or inhibited.
6. You are tired, even washed-out.
7. You feel inferior, worthless or you have undeserved feelings of guilt.
8. You can't think and concentrate properly anymore, and lack decision.
9. You feel desperate and may have fantasies about suicide.

Source: *American Psychiatric Association. Diagnostic and Statistical Manual of Mental Disorders* 5th Edition.

Studies show that depression has increased tenfold worldwide in the past century.[18] Eight percent of the Dutch of twelve years or older themselves indicated in 2014 that they were having a depression or had had one in the past year. That corresponds to over a million people. Women are more likely to have a depression than men: nine percent of women versus six percent of men. Depressions seem to occur most often in middle age. One in ten forty- to fifty-year-olds indicates they were depressed over

18 Martin Seligman, *Authentic Happiness: Using the New Positive Psychology to Realize Your Potential for Lasting Fulfillment*, VS, 2004, blz. 64-65

the past year.[19] The figures do not lie and it is getting worse. Among students, depression is also becoming more common, whereas this should pre-eminently be a group that is discovering life and all its pleasures.[20] And in ten years' time the number of young people reporting to the doctor with depression complaints has tripled.[21] Contrary to what is commonly assumed, depression is much less a genetic than an experiential problem.[22] And at the same time as the increase in depression the use of antidepressants has also increased. Even if one has been treated, it appears that people may relapse into their old problems, and with depression this happens regularly. More relapse is observed after drug therapy than after psychotherapy. Medication ultimately only works for a (very) limited group and worldwide new ideas on how to deal with the 'new flu' are worked on with might and main. Newspapers[23] even call for solutions to this steadily growing problem, but the use of medicines continues to increase.

19 CBS (Centraal Bureau for Statistics, Dutch Central Agency of Statistics): *More than 1 million Dutch had depression*, 25 January 2016

20 Chris Wind, *Jong, somber en verdrietig: depressie tijdens studie* (*Young, gloomy and sad: depression during study*), Hanzemag.nl, 26 February 2015

21 Gripopjedip.nl ('Manage your dip')

22 Michael Yapko, *Hypnosis And The Treatment Of Depressions*, Brunner/ Mazel, New York, 1992, blz. 3-4

23 *Psychotherapie helpt maar matig tegen depressie* (*Psychotherapy only helps moderately against depression*), Trouw, 2 March 2010

Summary

The figures do not lie: Three hundred and fifty million people suffer from a form of depression. It is not for nothing that depression is called the new flu. Antidepressants are increasingly prescribed and often this is the only treatment plan. But about what exactly depression is, there is more ambiguity than we generally realize. Depression is a commonly known term of which we think we know everything. But our thinking about depression is coloured with assumptions. What assumptions we have about depression and the problems that this entails will become clearer in the next chapters.

6.
The opposite of depression

How profoundly assumptions and suppositions have influenced our thinking about depression hasn't become clear to me until the past ten years. I could tell just like every other person what the characteristics of depression are: being gloomy and sad for a long time, having had enough of it, maybe bad sleep etcetera.

But rarely is what we know about depression questioned, it's a given. Researched, acknowledged and that is final. My fellow teachers, coaches, doctors and psychologists do not seem to question this either. Does anyone ever wonder what that DSM list really tells us? This list gives the hallmarks of a disease and that disease is called depression. Treatment protocols and plans that have originated from this list I knew and they seemed good as well. Until I began to watch depression through a coach's eyes. In this chapter I will show that there is no solution for depression within the current way of thinking. Depression is a problem much is said about. But what do you strive for when you feel depressed? That is vague to say the least...

'If you don't know where you want to go, you can't get there either.'

The difference between therapy and coaching

That there is distinction between therapy and coaching is not clear to everyone. Many psychologists also call themselves coach and many coaches also do therapy. However, the methods and the manner of working are indeed different and therefore the approach too. Whereas therapy focuses more on the problem, its cause and coming to grips with it, coaching focuses more on what someone wants to achieve, its future effects and how to get there fastest. Therapy is therefore broader and more general and more problem-oriented, whereas coaching is more focused, goal- and solution-oriented. In therapy coming to terms is central, while in coaching centre stage is occupied by eliminating the blockages that are in the way of achieving your goal. These blockages often lie in ideas and beliefs of the past and often unconsciously hinder one's progress.

While I was working with client John (in the period I felt depressed myself) I asked myself a central question: 'What do you want when you are depressed. What do you want then? What is your goal when you are depressed? And what is your goal when you work with a depressed person?' To my great frustration, I didn't get any clarity about that. Not with regard to my client and not with regard to myself either.

In a good coach-training course, you will learn a range of techniques to work with all kinds of issues in a solution-oriented way. You will learn to effectively set goals, make contact and think in a problem-solving manner. And depending on your training and curiosity, you can pick up techniques to work with pessimism, negativity, self-esteem, confidence and even forgiveness. You can apply strategies to become more solution-oriented, learn to think strategically, communicate better and cope with uncomfortable emotions, and you can facilitate vision and sense of purpose and so on. But gloom and dejection, that's still the domain of psychologist and psychiatrist. Both I and the many colleagues I inquired with would work with dejection in the coaching way: set goals and then do something with pessimism and with all the related problems that are to be expected when you go down the list. However, this did not work, something was missing. Every goal I set together with my client John was as it were too small to be able to work effectively with his problem, as if we were working with a part but not the whole. We did not get at the essence of his state of mind. John himself also seemed to jump at every goal without any long-term results. I didn't understand that and whatever I did and whoever I asked, everyone, from coach to GP and psychologist, had his or her own idea about this, but nobody had a satisfactory answer.

As I said before, in that same period I myself was also down and didn't do anything about it, something I didn't understand at all. I, with so much knowledge and experience, had helped people with the most complex issues and did nothing about my own situation. A kind of total passivity had come over me. I was amazed by this. It was not as if I could not do anything or was so hopeless and therefore wasn't doing anything, no, I was not in the slightest interested in doing anything.

Looking back it is a fascinating experience; and just like I was not interested in changing my own situation, I also found no answers to the question: 'To what destination do I want to help my depressed client get on track at the end of the day?' At the same time, I started to wonder what my lack of interest and my inability were about and what would be a comprehensive goal for John to give him a direction to escape from his problem. Setting an ultimate goal is always necessary in coaching. Because if you don't know where you want to go, how can you get there?

The opposite of depression

That's why I wondered if there was a kind of opposite of depression. Just as the opposite of uncertain is self-confident or certain; of sad, happy; of 'out of your strength' to 'in your strength'. As I described in my personal story I found out, after my search in literature and on the Internet, that there is no opposite of depression.

I enquired with all my clients, colleagues and participants in my trainings. Everyone was able to describe depression to a greater or lesser extent, but no one could name the opposite. While precisely that state, the ultimate goal, is so important. Could that be the reason I was so utterly uninterested in doing anything at all about my situation? If you have no idea where you want to go and can only refer to your problem, you cannot do anything but go back to where you are. I simply didn't understand and started to wonder how this is possible. The answer I call *DSM thinking*[24], after *the* handbook for psychiatric disorders: *Diagnostic and Statistical Manual of Mental disorders.*

By DSM thinking I mean that standardized assumptions and ideas have arisen from the long-term usage of knowledge from the *Diagnostic and Statistical Manual of Mental Disorders* (DSM). These assumptions and ideas have become part of our thinking to such an extent that we rarely ever or even never question them, for the simple reason that it doesn't occur to us.

Summary
The DSM list tells us something about the symptoms of depression, but nothing about what state of mind you want to achieve to make you feel better. What is actually your aim when you feel depressed? This question is very important if you feel dejected or want to counsel dejected people. Depression is recognized by everyone, but the opposite of depression is unknown. How is it possible that, when talking about depression, we don't know what we want to achieve? I give that fixed way of thinking the name 'DSM thinking'. In the subsequent chapter I am going to have a closer look at it.

---

24 With 'the DSM thinking' I refer only to depression and no other psychiatric syndromes described in the DSM.

7.
DSM-Thinking

The handbook for psychiatric disorders, *Diagnostic and Statistical Manual of Mental Disorders,* or the DSM has been used since 1952 to assemble our mental-emotional problems, conveniently arranged in one volume. The DSM has made possible an overview in a confusing world of mental problems. However, apart from neatly arranging the psychological problems we can experience, the handbook has also caused problems. One of these problems is that we consider the knowledge in the DSM handbook as true. The government does so, the health insurers, employee insurance agencies, the Job Centre Plus, general practitioners do so, and people like you and me follow their lead.

Two major problems that arise from what I call the DSM thinking are that depression is supposed to be a disease and that the deviation from what we describe as normal is also a possible syndrome. For example, mourning after a loved one is deceased, and therefore feeling very down, is also described in the latest DSM version as being depressed. In this chapter I am bringing up for discussion whether depression is a disease, and I consider whether deviations from what can be rightfully called normal should be described as sickness. I understand that this chapter is a bit of gritting their teeth for some, because the DSM is not that inspiring. But read it anyway. Because once you understand how we see depression to date, doors to new insights are opened. The DSM thinking implies a number of assumptions that blur our view of depression and the consequences of this are greater than you would expect at first glance.

The origins of the DSM

When we talk about depression, we are soon talking about the DSM. This psychiatric handbook describes all the commonly occurring mental illnesses and it influences our thinking about depression more deeply than you would initially suspect. The first edition (DSM-I) from 1952 described a hundred and twelve disorders, and the latest (DSM-V) describes more than three hundred and fifty disorders. The DSM was created because there was a sizeable confusion of tongues internationally. In mental health care, complaints and symptoms are often described in a vague, complex and incoherent manner, and moreover the assessment of a problem strongly depends on the assessor's expertise.

For example, terms like psychosis and depression were confused by different authors, interpreted differently and locally coloured. That is why there was a need to create order in the chaos. The goal of the DSM was to bring more unity in determining what problem a patient might have. This is the way the DSM has been created and, although there is now international consensus in psychiatry about the various disorders, the descriptions remain a rough yardstick.[25]

In a slump or depressed

Colloquially, the term depressed is quickly used when you are in a slump or down. However, one speaks of a depressive disorder or clinical depression when there is a persistent depressive mood, which is present almost daily and throughout most of the day. This manifests itself in the reduction of interest and pleasure. In that case you will meet five to nine criteria as described in the DSM (see Chapter 5).

25 Wikipedia: DSM

DSM-V describes depression as follows:
Depression is when you are unusually gloomy for more than two weeks and/or do not enjoy anything anymore. This is accompanied by other complaints, such as sleep disorders, decreased appetite, low energy, fatigue, concentration problems, indecision, inertia, physical restlessness, guilt feelings, excessive thoughts about death or suicide.

A distinction is made in the severity of the problems depending on the extent to which your functioning is limited (see Chapter 5):

Severely limited: You have seven to nine symptoms, these are intense and you suffer daily from them, in such a way that this is not manageable for you and that your symptoms hinder your social functioning.
Moderately Limited: You have between five and nine symptoms and you are hindered in your daily functioning. Your dejection has a significant influence on your general experience of happiness and daily functioning.
Slightly Limited: Then you have five of the nine symptoms and you suffer somewhat under them. You feel you are down but can function, although you find yourself less social than before. Your daily functioning has deteriorated to a lesser extent.[26]

The problem with DSM-thinking
Although the nine criteria of depression mentioned in DSM-V make it appear otherwise, it is well known among psychiatrists that there is much more ambiguity about depression than one is made to believe. There are ideas about what depression is and about the general symptoms there is fairly good agreement as well. However, there is still no researcher who has been able to diagnose clinically what is actually going on with a depressed person. No exact brain areas have yet been established that explain

26 Mens en Samenleving (People and Society): Psychology, *Depression symptoms DSM-V: Features and treatment*, November 2011

why depression shows itself the way it does. Also, no substances that determine whether you are depressed or not, have been identified with certainty in the brain. Moreover, there is no agreement on how depression arises. This is quite shocking when you consider that on the basis of the descriptions in the DSM it is decided what someone suffers from and how it should be treated.

The DSM thinking creates a number of subtle problems, not in the least because we assume that the information in the DSM is factual. Among other things, it is a given that depression is a disease, but is it?

Disease or symptom?
How do you know if a mental-emotional problem is a disease or a normal reaction to your living conditions? It is quite a difference to see a problem as a disease or as a manifestation of a problem in your life. Worse still, it seems that every deviation of the happiness standard is now classified as a disease. Here are five examples to illustrate this:

ADHD occurs less in France where they don't use the DSM.
In recent years there has been more and more criticism of the DSM and not in the last place from their own circle. More and more deviations from the norm are described as mental disorders. You can already see this in the huge increase in disorders described in the handbook since 1952. The boundaries are steadily pushed back in order to map out how many types of deviations from the norm there actually are. In France, ADHD among young people is significantly less prevalent than in the US. The French haven't been using the DSM for some years now and have their own psychiatric handbook: CFTMEA (*Classification Française des Troubles Mentaux de L'Enfant et de L'Adolescent*). The focus of the CFTMEA is on determining the underlying psychological causes of the symptoms, not on

finding pharmacological stopgaps to mask symptoms, as the DSM does.[27]

This brings us directly to a major problem of DSM thinking. The DSM describes symptoms and relates the classifications to medication. In other words, the manner of thinking of DSM focuses mainly on finding and providing medicines as a solution to the person's suffering. The handbook does not investigate the underlying causes of the psychological and emotional problems that people can be afflicted with. Remember that the DSM is the psychiatric handbook for diagnostics and that a psychiatrist is a doctor who specializes in mental illness. Diseases, as we all know, are dealt with in roughly two ways: we remove the disease by cutting something out or off, putting together and repairing, or prescribing medicines. Granted, this works pretty well in many cases when we are talking about physical problems, but does it work when it comes to mental emotional suffering? That explains why the writers are so keen to identify the symptoms in the DSM and define them as sickness. Only then you can prescribe medication for it.

Seeing suicide as a disease provides money for research

From this disease-thinking surprising things issue. In the article '*Alarm om toename zelfdodingen*' (*Alarm over increasing suicides*)[28], professors André Aleman and Damien Denys sound the alarm. 'If nothing happens, the number of suicides in our country continues to increase at an alarming rate. It is therefore necessary to outline a joint approach as soon as possible.' The solution? Both professors advocate that suicide should be recognized as a separate disorder. Why do doctors want suicide to be recognized as disorder? If a problem is recognized as a mental illness, it can be included in the DSM manual and

---

27 Marilyn Wedge, *Why French kids don't have ADHD*, Psychology Today, March 2012
28 Arianne Mantel, *Alarm om toename zelfdodingen* (*Alarm over increasing suicides*), Telegraaf, 22 mei 2014

research money will be made available by the government. Until then, no such luck. That's great if you really have to do with a disease. But what if, for example, suicide is not a disease, but the symptom of someone's problem, that he or she isn't able to solve? By declaring it a disease, we eventually have to revert again to the medical solutions: cut out or medicines... What if we would see depression again as a symptom complex??[29] A symptom complex which says something about one's life, experiences, upbringing, events.

'Depression isn't a disease!'

Depression is a western syndrome

From the DSM circle, too, are heard some notable criticisms. Professor Christopher Dowrick (United Kingdom) argues that there is no consensus in psychiatry about what depression is and what it exists of. He argues that depression might be a western culture-bound syndrome, a way to express tension and discomfort and so ask for help. But once a condition is in DSM-V, it is confirmed in the eyes of many without any dissenting opinion. He says about this: 'In Western society we have developed an ethics of happiness in which deviations from the happiness ideal are seen as an indications of sickness.'

Scientific research without context

If a disease is in such a leading handbook, we assume that it is based on thorough research. After all, our scientific climate is put together like this, we assume. Nothing is further from the truth, as evidenced by the BBC2 documentary *The Trap: What Happened to Our Dream of Freedom* from 2007 in which Dr. Robert Spitzer admits that the DSM classifications are not based on scientific research and that the diagnoses do not have a scientific basis. He

29 Leaving aside genetically and otherwise medically established depression.

can know, after all he has co-operated on the last but two versions of the DSM. He recounts: 'We made estimates of the extent to which mental disorders would occur on the basis of descriptions, without considering that many of these conditions could very well be normal reactions and no disturbances at all. That is the problem: we didn't look at the context in which these conditions occurred.'

Normal states of mind as disorders
Psychiatrist Allen Frances (the chief compiler of DSM-IV) tells Marie-Anne Zuidhof of '*De kennis van nu' (Today's knowledge*) that the new DSM is radically shifting the boundaries between crazy and normal. Completely normal states of mind are now disorders. PMS, mourning, restless children, all of them are disorders now. 'For the pharmaceutical industry this is great progress because normal people can now become even more stuffed with medicines.'[30] For example, to the latest version, DSM-V, are added quite a few new syndromes, and one of them is mourning. But how do you differentiate grief due to mourning from other forms of grief? Mourning is always accompanied by grief and often by dejection, but labelling mourning as depression is new.

Imagine the following scenarios:
A woman has been happily married for thirty years and comes home and finds her husband dead. She is in shock and gets increasingly sad in the days after. She is full of disbelief as to the loss of her beloved, she cries at every word about her husband and starts sleeping badly, eats badly, she finds nothing worthwhile anymore and can no longer concentrate. She wishes that she had died, too. After fifteen days, the phenomena are still present and her GP prescribes her antidepressants. The doctor does something most of us would think weird, prescribe medication for something that everyone would say is a normal response to loss. Until recently, mourning

30 Marie-Anne Zuidhof, *De duivelse DSM-V* (*the devilish DSM-V*), De kennis van nu (Today's knowledge), NPO, 24 May 2013

was not included in the DSM and therefore no mental disorder. Now it is. Suddenly mourning, or coping with bereavement, is a mental disorder. Instead of forming a normal aspect of being human, mourning has become a disease.

Now imagine the following scenario: A woman comes home and finds her husband in bed with her best friend, and this after a fine marriage of thirty years. Her husband indicates he is going to leave her. She is in shock and gets increasingly sad in the days after. She is full of disbelief as to the behaviour of her beloved and best friend. She cries with every word about her husband and starts sleeping badly, eats badly, finds nothing worthwhile anymore and can no longer concentrate. She wishes she was dead. After fifteen days, the phenomena are still present and her GP prescribes her antidepressants.

This last example has for thirty years been a reason to pronounce someone depressed according to the DSM criteria, even though in both examples there is immense grief; There is no underlying difference in both experiences. In fact, there has never been any clue to distinguish mourning and depression from one another. So how do we know how to deal with this problem? When all is said and done, it seems we can't tell.

Without us realizing it, the DSM thinking has penetrated deep into our collective subconscious. Since the first edition of the DSM, the handbook has been in the bookcase of the GP. And when you went to the doctor and you had a mental-emotional problem, then the GP grabbed the DSM edition of that moment. Patients went home to tell in which disease category they fell. Mentally disturbed people in films get their character traits from the DSM classifications. Documentaries about human behaviour have to meet at least the symptoms associated with the medical picture. The government has already for years acknowledged the expertise described in the DSM. Health insurers, occupational physicians and re-integration centres all want to have a DSM classification to justify themselves.

Therefore, our way of thinking about depression has been strongly influenced by unconscious assumptions that we have adopted from the DSM. These assumptions which, to say the least, are misleading, result in a search for wrong solutions and treatment methods within a medical framework.

Summary

The two major problems with DSM thinking are: 1. The DSM thinking classifies a mental-emotional problem as a disease, while in many cases of dejection you cannot speak of a disease but, on the other hand, of a natural reaction to experiences in one's life. 2. In addition, deviations from the happiness standard are classified as illness in the DSM. Moreover, it is important to have a mental-emotional problem recognized as a disease because only then research funds are made available. This medicalization of mental-emotional problems has major consequences. Unfortunately, a medical interpretation of a mental emotional problem can only suggest medical solutions: operating or medicines. Without our being aware of it, we have grown up in a DSM culture. Our thinking about depression is linked up with the list of nine criteria in the handbook. In the next chapter I will explain why it is that assumptions influence our thinking and actions so strongly and what the paramount assumptions are that have created the DSM thinking about dejection.

8.
The five assumptions about depression

In order to understand more thoroughly the process that we just accept things on hearsay, we go back to the human mind. It is necessary to ask ourselves how people create their reality and how our cultural frameworks emerge, the ideas we embrace as a group. Moreover, we want to know how our assumptions about depression have arisen. Thus, we kill three birds with one stone. On the one hand, it becomes clear how we can act unconsciously from assumptions and, on the other hand, it explains how as an individual you create your reality. This is important because we are slowly but surely going to explore the inner landscape of dejection. It begins with a glimpse into our human mind. Resulting from this, I sum up the five biggest problems that arise from DSM thinking. These five points blur what it is all about with dejection and contribute to the lack of clarity about what to do, by which your striving for happiness becomes frustrated. You can understand depression much better when you get rid of the assumptions that have formed your thinking about depression.

In our minds, two things play an elementary role in how we create our reality. These points have a lot to do with each other and affect each other. In this chapter, I discuss the first point 'meaning'. The other item 'reflexivity' will be discussed in Chapter 10.

> ## 'Meaning is what distinguishes us from each other, it is our only remaining instinct.'
> *Michael Hall*

What does that mean?

We are meaning-assigning beings, just think about it.[31] We assign meaning to all our observations, to someone's look, to the choice of clothes you make in the morning and whether you find a website beautiful or unsightly. Also, when you have a look at yourself in the mirror and have thoughts about how your hair or your body looks, even about your feelings of that moment. Assigning meaning is so primary that in many cases we are completely unaware of the fact that we are assigning meaning. Because perception and significance are linked as quick as lightning to one another, we don't question many of the things we should be questioning. Why? Because some things are 'just the way they are'. We often experience our world as a given, firmly established. The conclusions we draw are so obvious to ourselves because they feel true. But is that so? Are things 'the way they are, just like that'? Are our conclusions true just like that?

Accepting ideas as true

The fact that we adopt ideas without questioning them is a special phenomenon and has its roots in how we humans create our group feeling. To illustrate how we adopt ideas that were sometimes conceived generations ago, I'm going to make a small trip to the core of our group feeling: our culture. 'The emergence of a culture is the answer of a group to how to survive in a threatening situation', according to anthropologist Edward Tylor.[32] As culture

31 Michael Hall, *Meta-States: Mastering the Higher States of Your Mind*, US, 2000
32 Wassili Zafiris, Ben Steenstra, *IK BEN niet alleen op de wereld* (to be published in English as *Meaningful Profit*), 2011, p. 83

comes from cultivating and means as much as tilling the land, the threatening situations Tylor referred to are the threats of nature. Historically, we have armed ourselves against all kinds of natural threats. We Dutch have built dikes against water and the pilgrims in America carried weapons to defy the dangers of the wilderness. If a solution is effective against a threat, the solution becomes a rule. Thus, the right to bear arms in the US has become a rule and so is allowed. But the rule that once ensured that the group of pilgrims could survive is a problem many years later. The American culture in which the possession of arms is contained in the constitution is the cause of many deaths, which might never occur if weapons were banned. Let's take this description of what a culture is and how ideas are passed without discussion to future generations and combine it with what we know about depression.

As soon as we are in system that is functioning, we are not so easily going to bring up previously made assumptions for discussion. The same is true for the DSM-thinking. The need to bring together all these different ideas about mental problems in a clear overview was a genuine need, but the ensuing drawbacks we have also got into the bargain. We have been contented ourselves with the answers to the question of what depression is and rarely bring them under discussion. It looks like we are not questioning this because we don't know any better. Admittedly, this is difficult because our entire system is designed in keeping with the DSM thinking.

Why is it so difficult for us to rise above those frameworks? What keeps us from researching things once more and questioning assumptions? Some things are just the way they are... aren't they? We live in a world of meaning. Meaning that we create ourselves and continually reinvent, but also meaning that has been passed on to us by previous generations, scientists, institutes and political systems.

Five assumptions of DSM thinking

DSM thinking has also created a number of assumptions. What we know about depression is strongly influenced by this. The hidden assumptions, ideas and premises of the DSM have influenced people suffering from (chronic) gloom, therapists, researchers, policymakers and ordinary happiness seekers like you and me, without us being fully aware of it. To understand depression, it is necessary to give up the following assumptions:

1. Depression is a disease.
2. The cause is in our brains.
3. The symptoms are the problem.
4. Naming the problem is more important than naming the solution.
5. If you are not normal, you are sick.

1. Depression is a disease.
Although this has already been discussed to some extent, I still would like to emphasize that psychiatry sees depression as a disease. Disease-thinking implies a medicinal (antidepressant) solution to this problem (because operating isn't an option). That is, to say the least, dubious with respect to the largest group of depressives in whom no medical cause of their suffering has been established. The medical approach is used for the entire group and not only for the select group in which a medical cause has been determined. It is a 'substances' approach, which assumes that something is (temporarily) out of order and that replenishing the right substances (antidepressants) is the Holy Grail. I also notice that clients have for years been asked only one question during their weekly visits to the psychiatrist: 'Should the dosage be up or down?' Disease-thinking implies that an illness is the cause, as a virus causes a flu. As will be shown in point 2, this is a very special conclusion indeed.

2. The cause is in our brains.
Oddly enough, there is a lot of ambiguity about the genesis of depression. There are different theories, and

depending on which one you adhere to, you are inclined to one explanation or another. There are experts who go for the resilience theory. The idea is that if your resilience is reduced, you are more likely to become depressed. The DSM is fairly unambiguous about this, and in particular it looks at the physiological causes: brain nuclei that produce too few of the right substances or brain nuclei that produce too much of the not-right substances or a combination of these. All of this is possible and if you do therapy as a psychiatrist, neurologist or physiologist, or do research, then of course you look at a problem this way. Your background influences your perception, which makes sense. The DSM also does not make any attempt to identify underlying psychosocial causes. The handbook isn't really equipped for that. However, unambiguousness in how depression in most cases arises (apart from the physiological explanations) would make sense. Especially when you want to be able to counsel effectively or want to understand your problem.

3. The symptoms are the problem.
The handbook describes only symptoms of depression, what they look like; the things that the chronically gloomy person himself can describe. The DSM describes symptoms and the medicinal solution. The two worlds described are the outward world of the symptoms and the physiological world of the molecules. Yet in between there is another world, the world of the experience of the person in question. We all know that describing the symptoms is not the same as describing the disease. Symptoms are the outward characteristics. The symptoms tell us nothing about how a depressed person thinks, what they experience, how they draw conclusions or look at themselves and the world. It is only an ascertainment of what can be perceived. For us, that is what depression is. The list from the DSM.

4. Naming the problem is more important than formulating the solution.

We have learned to think about depression as a disease without a solution. In our language there is no solution for the depressive state that everyone recognizes. Something like this: 'Oh, you're feeling down, then, of course, you want... this or that.' There is no or very little insight into what the depressive really wants. The solution is not in our collective consciousness. To refer to a problem without a solution will cause you to hang around in the 'neighbourhood of your problem', a perpetual wandering without any reason to go on a trip. Meticulously verifying the problem without meticulously deciding on the solution is quite remarkable when you come to think of it.

5. If you are not normal, you are sick.

Deviations from the happiness norm we have come to see as an indication of sickness. We have sick or normal, and, as has become even clearer in the latest DSM version, more and more manifestations of maladjusted behaviour are labelled as disease. How matter-of-course the DSM thinking is became apparent last January when a new client called me, asking if I could help her with her feelings of dissatisfaction. Her psychologist, by whom she had been treated for some time, could not do anything more for her: 'You don't have a 'DSM-like something' madam, so I can't do anything for you.' Both the woman and the psychologist were happy with this. But what is normal? And to see deviations 'from the normal' as disease... Is that, of all things, a solution? Then 'just being happy' is a far better option. Or isn't it? The happiness frame causes us to look for abnormalities, and to label them as not all right and even diseased. The enormous societal need for happiness contributes to judging deviations from what is generally considered normal behaviour. However, that same need for happiness is based on the wrong happiness goal. Wrong because the happiness we aim at is unattainable. My research shows that going for unachievable targets is precisely a trigger for gloom. The fact is, these happiness targets are 'too far away'; outside the experience world of a depressed person and very unspecific. I'll tell you more about that later.

'We have learned to think about depression as a disease without a solution.'

Now, the DSM-thinking is not the fault of the psychiatrists who have written the DSM. Our opportunistic brain (see Chapter 1) may be prone to quickly want to overlook our problems for a new opportunity. The medicinal approach may be a part of that opportunism, 'a pill and finished!' Then we don't need to tackle and change anything. The idea that happiness can be achieved in seven steps is a result of this opportunism. The less happiness we experience the greater the gap between where we are and where we hope to be. This causes discouragement because something unachievable we give up over time.

From a different perspective
As you have seen, the five depicted assumptions create important constraints in how we think about depression and how we could change depression. In order to be able to view dejection from a different perspective, we need to find answers to the limitations that the DSM thinking has given us. Below is stated what needs to be done in order to be capable of being open to new ideas about what depression is, to find solutions from within other frameworks.

We are going to examine the assumptions to find new solutions:

1. **Depression is a disease**. It is important to get dejection out of the disease model so that we can realize again that our mental-emotional problems are in some way reactions to circumstances of our lives (see Chapter 9 *The onset of*

depression). The question we wish to ask is: If depression is not a disease, what is it?

2. The cause is in our brains. Without having to let go of the physiological assertions about the onset of depression, it makes sense to go and look for the different living conditions that cause dejection. This gives handles for a new approach that is closer to the inner perception of the depressed person (see Chapter 9). We are going to investigate which living conditions can cause depression.

3. The symptoms are the problem. We have to separate the problem and its appearance from each other again. That gives us the ability to perceive more objectively and to learn without bias from our dejection. This means that we want to investigate what a dejected person is experiencing inside. Because by becoming more accurate in this, we get crucial clues about how happiness can come back in our lives. In Chapter 10 *Your inner world is changing* and Chapter 11 *Dark Landscape* I separate the symptoms from the problem and explore the inner landscape of depression to discover from the inner experience what depression is.

4. Naming the problem is more important than naming the solution. We need to turn this problem around, because in this case we need the solution instead of the problem. This means that a new vision is needed about what state of mind you want to pursue when you feel depressed. In Chapter 12 we describe what is really important: what you want to achieve when you are depressed.

5. If you are not normal you are sick. Deviating from the happiness standard implies that you are sick. Instead of taking this as true, we have to ask ourselves whether we have the right pursuit of happiness. I think we must pursue a different kind of happiness. A brand of happiness that is closer to our experience. A brand of happiness that gives us insight into what to do when we are stuck in dejection and indefinable feelings. Chapter 12 makes clear what that happiness is and what the benefits of another going for happiness are.

Summary

We are meaning-ascribing beings and take up meanings from previous generations. We have also done that with how we think about depression. The five assumptions underlying how we think about depression are: depression is a disease; the cause of depression is in the brain; the symptoms are the problem; the problem is more important than the solution and if you are not normal, you are sick. These ideas have a great influence on how we think about depression, but also on how we think depression comes into being and how we can solve it. But what happens if we were to get rid of these assumptions? In Chapter 9 I embark on a discussion of the first two assumptions (depression is a disease, the cause of depression is in the brain).

9.
The onset of depression

Defining a medical problem as disease can be very helpful in treating that disease. To approach a general mental-emotional problem as a disease is too limited an approach in many cases, because human beings are not separate from the context they live in. In this chapter I first of all discuss why the assumption 'depression is a disease' is not complete. So, if depression is not a disease, what is it? I will also show that causes of depression are not just in the physiological brain (chemical substances), but that three causes can be pointed out that, in a particular combination, trigger dejection. The causes of depression are loneliness, a changing self-image and adversity.

Disease versus interpretation
As has been said, there is no ambiguity as to how depression originates and, depending on the background of the researcher, other causes of how depression arises are put forward. From a pharmacological perspective, the focus is on which substances are missing, whether too many are present or how connections may be disrupted. This approach stems from disease-thinking about depression and blames chemical substances and brain nuclei for all misery.

Since our moods change and can only change because chemicals are created, not created or inhibited, it is quite logical that something affects the brain nuclei, neurotransmitters and all related physiological elements.

But to identify these elements as the only cause of the depressive state is too narrow. The interaction with our environment requires continual effective adaptation of our internal environment, in other words: the right chemicals need to be created in order to activate moods that help us respond in the right way.

'Humans remain beings that in interaction with their environment need the most appropriate meaning in order to activate the most effective physiological response in themselves.'

One could say that how we attribute meaning to the interactions with our environment determines how our internal environment responds to this outer environment. For example, if we interpret an experience as something beautiful and valuable, our internal environment will react to it and activate those brain nuclei and substances that awaken the nice feelings in us. Then we will feel fine and warm. If we interpret an event as threatening or dangerous, our neurology will activate the appropriate substances that ensure that we alert and protect ourselves (and may feel tense or angry). If this were not to take place, we might put ourselves at risk. So must we respond to it appropriately.

Wrong response

Now, we all know that our reaction pattern is often not adequate. And in choosing the right response in relation to events in the world, errors can occur. For example, people may be afraid of spiders, even terrified, without any spider near. We also know that most spiders we encounter are not

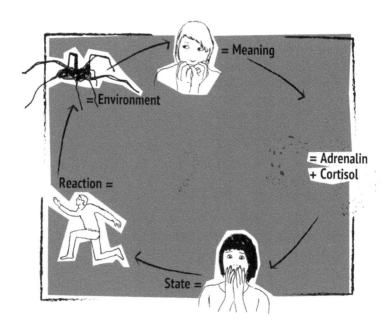

dangerous at all, and what could a spider do anyway... Yet, some of us are very afraid of something that really needn't be feared. So, our personal interpretation does not have to correspond to what is presented to us at all. All the same, our interpretation causes our brain to create chemicals and activates nuclei, which alerts us and makes us want to run away, for example from a spider that is not there at all.

'The causes of depression are loneliness, a changing self-image and adversity.'

Intervening at the level of brain nuclei and chemical substances through medication may be sensible in a number of cases. This way you change your physiological reaction and, if you are lucky, also, after some time, the meaning you assign to events and experiences. Nevertheless, a physiological explanation of a phenomenon is, on its own merits, a very limited representation of what happens to a human being in interaction with his or her world. To start with, it could be that in exceptional cases the chemicals and nuclei do not work well, just as you can be born with a spina bifida. Due to developmental circumstances and genetics, part of your physiology does not function as it should. An approach with a 'disease spectacle' can be extremely effective. It could even be that through an accumulation of experiences and events, brain nuclei and chemicals react immediately. It is also possible that deeply affecting experiences, such as trauma, interfere with physiology. In spite of all these possible scenarios, humans remain beings who in interaction with their environment need the most appropriate meaning in order to activate the most effective physiological response in themselves. Therefore, your interpretation of experiences, events, feelings and memories is essential. Your interpretative style is largely picked up from previous experiences or examples. In a depressed person, the interpretative style has got so disturbed that they are in a deep state of gloom. The question is: What is it caused by?

2. The causes of depression

There are three causes that trigger a chronically gloomy mindset: loneliness, changing self-image, adversity. A combination of two random causes is often sufficient to trigger a depressive state of mind.

Armageddon

A wonderful example that fully matches my findings on how depression arises are the experiences of Giles Andreae (1966). This writer, who was in the English top ten bestseller list in 2009 with five books, became depressed overnight.

Giles describes his experiences in a very evocative way in *I lost the gift of joy for a while* (the Times online, November 23, 2009). Without realizing it, he is talking about the causes of depression: The loneliness he experiences, how his self-image suddenly changes, and how setback after setback causes his future perspective to disappear: 'It was half past eleven on a Saturday morning, at the low point of the recession and an important contract didn't get through... in the City in London news about an impending Armageddon kept cropping up. While I was going upstairs to turn on the bath it was like I heard my brain break. An hour later I was in the hospital.'

LONELINESS

My research and counselling people for more than twenty-five years have shown that connection and the feeling of belonging are essential to us. When we don't belong and don't feel connected, we become lonely, then we feel alone. Loneliness is a trigger for the emergence of depressed feelings. Especially the loss of family, loved ones and friends plays an important part. It is important for us to experience the deeply felt awareness of having a family and that this family is there for you, that this family cares for you, provides you with security and warmth. The loss, whether or not actual, of family, loved ones and friends may be a cause of the onset of depressive feelings. The dominant thoughts you have then are: 'I am alone, abandoned...' , 'There is no one for me, no one who really understands me.' But also thoughts like: 'Others are not to be trusted', 'people are bad', play a great part in feelings of loneliness.

'...you realize that the rest of your life will be spent spinning alone, weightless, through the dark emptiness of space.'

Giles Andreae

You may be in a room with people, even acquaintances, family and loved ones around you and still feel lonely, alone. Often this has been preceded by years of slowly worsening loneliness. Maybe you didn't really regard this as too bad yourself, because there were plenty of reasons why it had worked out the way it had. 'That friend took me for a ride and that one too' and slowly you didn't enter into any serious friendships any more, and you developed underlying beliefs about people, such as 'people are not to be trusted anyway', 'in the end you will be deserted', 'nobody is favourably disposed towards you.' Also in the relationship sphere, experiences can be generalized about fidelity and infidelity, feeling understood or not by partners and loved ones, betrayal. In these cases, too, or together with the preceding example, one chooses at some point to remain distant from others. In a number of cases, my clients tell me that this feeling started or emerged early in their earliest youth. Not having a sense of belonging, being on the outside, not feeling loved or appreciated may all be experiences that strengthen those feelings of loneliness. Ultimately, they can lead to existential loneliness, the perception of being alone in the world. As if there is no proximity to other people. People who experience existential loneliness, have too great a mental distance to friends, loved ones, family and all people in the world to experience a sense of connection or belonging to them. The isolation often increases slowly but surely. Sadness about this is seldom expressed, or on the contrary, extremely, at moments someone is aware of how lonely they actually feel.

CHANGING SELF IMAGE

We generally thrive better when we are happy with ourselves and can rely on a stable identity. Identity problems are quite common; for example, uncertainty due to a limited sense of self-esteem is more prevalent than you might expect at first. What I found striking during my conversations with depressed clients was that their self-image had not changed gradually but unexpectedly and suddenly, in an almost dramatical manner. A sudden shake-up in your self-image can stir up dejection. Your self-image can change suddenly by, for example, an accident causing the loss of a limb, or a serious illness, but also, though less severe, if you have always defined yourself as a sportsman but can no longer practice your sport because your knee can't cope anymore. Or you get the sack and experience this as a slap in your face. You become fatter and don't recognize yourself in the mirror anymore. You do something you had never expected from yourself (you beat your wife) and more similar unexpected changes in how you experience yourself.

'...a growing sense of who 'me' is, has suddenly been completely voided. Dramatic? Yes. Terrifying? Absolutely.'

Giles Andreae

NOT RECOGNIZING YOURSELF ANYMORE

An about 35-year-old sportswoman comes to me and tells me that she hasn't been feeling happy for a long time. She has everything on track, she had a successful professional career as a sportswoman, which came to an end some years ago. She is full of ideas and begins to tell me that, although she has started a fairly successful new career, she cannot really be happy. Relationships do not work at all, and her life has also changed very much after her top-sports career. In the middle of our conversation she says while pointing at her body: 'You know

Wassili, this isn't me.' Her hands move up and down, pointing at her body. Once again she says: 'This isn't me, the other day I looked in the mirror and didn't see a sportswoman anymore; this isn't me. I did not feel happy as it was, but this...'

The (un)conscious experience in which there is a rift between the image you have always had of yourself and the sudden awareness that you no longer come up to that image of yourself is a shocking and seriously disruptive experience. The essence you have built your life around over the past few years is roughly disturbed. 'This isn't me', people often say as an expression of the confusion that lives in the person about his or her actual self, the self that can be seen, felt and experienced by anyone, and the inner experience of how the person has experienced himself or herself until then. This shock initiates depression in many cases.

ADVERSITY

Setbacks can cause intense emotions and the deeper the setback makes its way in, the more likely you are to develop a bleak perspective. I don't mean one big setback or a few little ones in succession. No, really the experience of constant adversity, things that are always going against you, people who treat you badly, financial problems you cannot solve and so forth.

My research shows that the adversity that may cause depression is not a one-of-a-kind incident. Often there have already been some setbacks in one or two important areas of life, like relationship or health. However, in the case of many clients the depressive feelings apparently arose the moment that several often unexpected setbacks took place at the same time. The bad luck does not necessarily have to be real. Yes, the bad luck is real in the person's perception, but objectively the misfortune can be small or not measurable. The person who suffers adversity has a problem with his or her resilience. When many setbacks take place, a hard-luck mindset arises, 'Just my luck', you hear yourself cry out. It is the experience that everything is going against you, and that, moreover, everything will keep going against you. The hard-luck mindset expects adversity as a given, 'You see', then becomes your favourite statement.

'Then, in August last year, a couple of things happened simultaneously. The value of the financial nest egg that I had built up over twenty years of successful writing plummeted — and we decided to move out of London, away from the home in which we had brought up our family for the previous ten years. The platform on which I had been standing had disappeared. Beneath it was simply an abyss.'

Giles Andreae

These three causes of depression are subtly related. Often, I see a feeling of loneliness which, for example by disappointment in friendships, gets truly visible for the first time, but has been nourished by a deeper loneliness, a loneliness that has arisen before in a person's life. A suddenly changing self-image can take place at any moment in your life, from changing jobs to giving birth to a child. Decreased powers of resistance to adversity you may have got from your upbringing, but some people also get disproportionately many setbacks to handle. The fascinating thing is that all these causes are not necessarily true in the actual world. I mean that people can also become depressed when they just experience these matters internally. They are experienced in the inner landscape, even without objectively occurring events that might trigger these causes. Dejection comes into being when at least two causes get together. Which two those are depends on the person; however, once two have been activated, the third often emerges by itself.

> 'When you have this... you lose all sense of proportion. You chant an endless, repetitive mantra of personal nihilism. And that's a very hard and frustrating thing for those around you to cope with.'
>
> *Giles Andreae*

Summary

It has been scientifically proven that there are chemical substances in our brain that trigger all manner of things in us and activate moods. Only, the question is whether our brain produces these chemicals just like that. Our interpretative style, the meaning we attribute to our experiences, has a huge influence on what substances are activated in us. You can go through things in your life in such a way that your manner of interpreting begins to change. Even in such a way that you begin to feel really unhappy. Although DSM-thinking explains the cause of depression from the physiology of our brains, my research shows that three causes can be pointed out that can trigger and aggravate dejection: loneliness, a changed self-image and misfortune. You become depressed if you live through two or more of these problems. Now it is special that the loneliness, setback or causes of a changing self-image do not have to happen objectively, but in the perception of the person they do happen. In order to understand how this works and to comprehend what you are experiencing inside when you feel dejected, I am going to discuss in the next chapter the third assumption about depression (the symptoms are the problem). For, if the symptoms are not the problem, what is the problem with dejection?

10.
Your inner world is changing

If we assume that symptoms are not the problem, what is the problem (assumption three, chapter 8)? Depression is a special state of mind. Particularly because it looks as if it is very difficult to understand why someone becomes depressed. The three causes described in the previous chapter give insight into what can cause dejection. However, they do not yet explain what depression is and what elements a depressive state of mind consists of. Only when you know how this state of mind is composed can you start thinking about how you could change the elements depression is made up of. In this chapter we will therefore consider what depression is and how a depressive gestalt can emerge layer by layer and part by part.

The invisible world we live in

From the three causes that trigger depression it appears that depression is not a disease but a unique composition of feelings, frameworks of thoughts and convictions. It is the final manifestation of a number of complex mental-emotional steps that take place in a person. The symptoms a dejected person has are not the problem, they are the manifestation of the problem. The depressive state of mind is the ultimate result of one's unique way of interpreting the world he or she has lived in until then. Classifying depression as a disease is a very reductionist way of analysing depression and makes us react to depression as if it were a thing in itself. A virus, a tumour, a bacterium, an element not belonging to the body, which we must tackle. The disease model simplifies the phenomenon of depression, for it is not a disease with its associated cause, it is the end product of a someone's meticulous mental-emotional steps and evaluations in relation to his or her life events, experiences, people, the world and themselves. Depression is a *gestalt* phenomenon! I'll explain that in a moment.

We can think about our thoughts and feel about our feelings.[33] In 2004 I was in San Diego and I watched the play-offs of the American men's beach-volleyball team. The winning team would go to the Olympic Games in Athens that year, so the last game was quite important. Afterwards, the winning team captain was interviewed. He was asked if he had been nervous at the start of the contest. While he was getting the microphone shoved under his nose, he replied after some doubting: 'Yeah, I was nervous, but I was calm about it.' Those words stunned me. That one sentence made me aware of something so fundamental, that I still don't understand why I had never heard it before. He was indeed nervous, but that was not the only thing. He was calm about it! Somewhere in his inner landscape he had done something that I then experienced as something magical. In his mind he had put calmness on top of his nervousness, and by doing so in that specific way, his nervousness was at his service. Just imagine how you feel when you feel nervous but calm about it. This combination of states of mind creates a peculiar new state of mind. To one it is excited alertness and to the other it is being fully present. Whatever it is to you, the nervousness does not work against you anymore, but is at your service. How different it would be when you are nervous but are annoyed about it or, for example, uncertain, then a completely different state of mind will probably arise. In that case, you may become angry or anxious, these new states of mind will take possession of you. We can think about our thoughts and evidently also feel about our feelings (calm about

33 This can be called a form of reflexivity: be able to think about acts, www.betekenis-definitie.nl. See also chapter 8 *The five assumptions about depression.*

nervous) and the unique interplay between these layers of thoughts and feelings is an important part of how we shape and create our world.

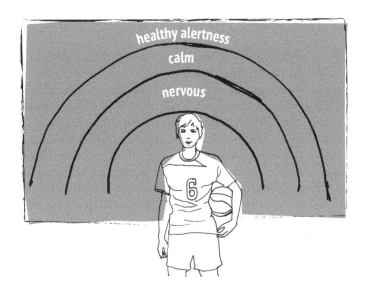

Layers of significance

Our inner world consists of a succession of inner reactions to thoughts and feelings. Judging our thoughts and feelings positively or negatively. We draw conclusions from our thoughts and feelings, which we subsequently draw conclusions from and develop ideas about, out of which consequently convictions will emerge. In the end all these reactions together mould something completely new. This new state of mind does not resemble any more the individual elements it is composed of. All this together constitutes a kind of transformer; you think you have to do with a car, but actually it is a robot as big as a building and when you see the building, you cannot imagine that it was originally a car.[34] The two are so far apart that you

34 After the film *Transformers*

cannot link them and yet they are made up of one another. The whole new thing that arises then you call a gestalt. The German psychologists Wolfgang Köhler and Max Wertheimer define a gestalt as a psychological overall picture, of which the whole is more than the sum of the constituent parts.[35]

It is the stratification of meaning in our thinking and feeling that causes us to like or not like something, find it beautiful or ugly, kind or unkind. We live in a world of meaning. On the one hand, I call that world the *Matrix*, after the film *The Matrix*, and on the other hand after Michael Hall's book of the same name.[36] The Matrix is the invisible world of meaning that someone is functioning in. Our Matrix determines whether we move towards or away from something. Our inner assessment style gives us insight into what we think is important, what goals we set, how we experience ourselves, whether we feel empowered or not, with whom we engage in what kind of relationships and with whom we don't. Whether we look forward or backward and in which worlds we can move freely. In other words, the Matrix is that place in which our thinking, feeling, our ideas and our unique way of looking at events and experiences are engendered.

All of these frameworks form layers over layers of meaning with which we create an inner landscape. Just like in the movie *The Matrix*, the inner landscape of a person is not the same as the landscape of the world around the person. On the basis of our invisible inner world, we begin to explore the world around us, and most of us function in it in a more or less reasonably happy and healthy manner. Until meanings are beginning to emerge that are less beautiful. And we experience things that create thinking frameworks that are not so healthy. When we have experiences with others which break or change our dreams

35 Wikipedia: Gestalt
36 Michael Hall, *The Matrix Model, The 7 Matrices of Neuro-Semantics,* USA, 2003

and visions, and in doing so, slowly but surely change our inner landscape...

> 'A neurotic is an expert in creating problems and a psychotic is an expert in devising unrealistic solutions.'
>
> *Unknown*

The depressive gestalt

To understand depression, we need to know something about how we shape, create and frame our inner world. With this knowledge we can better understand how depression arises, works and can be changed. The following coaching session with my client Elly is an example which unravels how those internal layers create a depressive gestalt.

REVEL IN SELF-PITY

Some time ago Elly came into my practice because of her depression. Although she had been under psychiatric treatment for nine years, she wanted to try something else. I got talking to her and Elly told me that she had been hospitalized at first because of a severe obsessive-compulsive neurosis. I had some inkling of what I was up against. It would be an in-depth conversation.

Elly didn't have an easy life. Medication for her neurosis to come into contact with blood, medication to eliminate the side effects of these drugs and years of cognitive and behaviour therapies that seemed to be somewhat effective until some time ago, when she woke up one morning and started crying and could not stop. Quickly the diagnosis of depression was made, because if you always cry, it seems quite logical. Even quicker, a pill was found that had to remedy the fault. I was somewhat amazed at this approach and began to ask her some questions about when she had woken up like this.

'So, when exactly did this start?'
'One morning I suddenly couldn't help crying and couldn't stop.'
'OK. I don't quite understand, you suddenly started crying?'
'Yes, I woke up and was unstoppable...'
'Had something happened?'
'No, nothing at all. I don't understand myself either.'
'What had happened then just before the moment you couldn't help crying?'
Silence.
'I mean just before the first tear?'
'Yes, then I had to think of my business that had gone bankrupt.'
'Your business?'
'Yes, I had a dog hair salon and after half a year I had to wind it up, because I didn't bring it off; just when I was getting back on track after that behaviour therapy for my obsessive-compulsive neurosis.'
'So you had a dog salon, could work independently after your behaviour therapy and then your business went bankrupt?'
'Yes, and I also got very fat after I had just lost fourteen kilos, fourteen kilos, mind you.'
'Jeez, that's all you need, what did that mean to you?'
'Well, that I had to disappoint my husband even more.'
'What exactly do you mean?'
'Well, we've been together for twelve years and for the last nine years it's been about me, I mean, for nine years I have been incapable of doing anything.'
'And you feel sad about that?'
'Yes.'
'Please explain, what is the relationship between your sadness and letting your husband down, your figure and your bankruptcy, right when things were looking up?'
'Well, I feel guilty.'

'What do you mean?'

'I actually feel guilty very often, I feel guilty about all sorts of things.'

'You might find me a bit silly, but I don't quite understand what you say, guilty?'

'Yes, I feel guilty about the fact that my business has gone bankrupt, that I am too fat, that I claim all my husband's attention and that I have not been able to function for years.'

'Oh, yes that's quite something, how do you feel about this now?'

'Sad, very sad.'

'Sadness that lingers all day?'

'Yes, I can't help crying all day.'

'So what you're actually saying is that you feel very sad about the fact that you feel guilty, and that means that your sadness is not the primary problem, but the result of your feelings of guilt... And that means you're getting medication for something that isn't the problem, but the symptom.'

Silence. Suddenly a total change in facial expression.

'Oh', she says, 'That's true, what you say is right, it's not one big mash I can't extricate myself from.'

'No, in fact, your sad feelings are your unique internal reaction to your feelings of guilt.'

'What would you call your attitude, the attitude you have towards yourself when you feel so sad about your guilty conscience?'

'Hmmm, I pity myself.'

'So self-pity. Yes, that would make me feel depressed, too. What is the effect of self-pity on the rest of your life?'

'Well, you don't see a future perspective anymore, you don't even see an opening anymore. No, it's just black then and you don't feel like moving forward anymore.'

'Because...?'

'Because it's no use, why move if you can't go anywhere, if it makes no sense...?'

'Yes, that seems quite pointless and awkward.'

'Yes, as if your life has no meaning, there is also so much misery in the world...'

Elly's depressive feelings evidently aren't for no reason. In order to not stop crying, Elly has drawn certain conclusions and passed certain judgments, she has evoked feelings and taken them as true. She ends up responding to all these internal reactions with self-pity, and that state of mind causes her to have no future perspective and causes her inner landscape to become dark. As she indicates herself, it has got 'just black'.

The depressed gestalt is an accurately composed landscape of our mind. A gestalt is a whole of behaviours, patterns, ways of processing information that cannot be explained from the independent parts. The unique interplay between all the states of mind creates a new phenomenon. Simply adding up all phenomena does not explain the end phenomenon. This means that there is something unpredictable in bringing together all these different elements. We all know this, because most of us have at times been angry about nothing or seen people who got angry for inexplicable reasons. Suddenly the person became angry or even furious, suddenly someone's temper and approach of a situation utterly changed. On the outside a fairly inexplicable phenomenon, but for the person in question a normal pattern.

'If you think about it logically, you would not expect or predict at all that two gases can produce a liquid element.'

Water as a gestalt?

Let's take a molecule, by way of comparison, to explain what a gestalt is. For example water, H_2O. A water molecule consists of atoms, namely two hydrogen atoms (H_2) and one oxygen atom (O). We know that hydrogen is a gas that can adopt liquid forms under high pressure and that oxygen surrounds us and we can breathe through oxygen.

Suppose we were to come on a planet and find H2 for the first time in its pure form as a gas. Then we wouldn't be able to predict, just like that, what would happen if we were to add another atom. On the contrary, at first we would probably not even think of another manifestation, certainly not one that is so radically different from the atoms themselves. We know that when we merge hydrogen and oxygen under the right conditions, H2O is produced, that elixir of life our body for the most part consists of. But could we have predicted it? Yes, we can explain it at the molecular level, but understand it completely? The coming into being of water is actually a huge surprise.

All in all, the new element water, which arises from the loose elements (gases) H2 and O2 is an inexplicable miracle. We cannot explain water from the bringing together of two gases and yet it has existed as long as we are here and far before. Water seems to have nothing more to do with all the loose parts. Suddenly, gas has become water. As if out of nowhere, an all-inclusive new structure has arisen. Water is a gestalt.

Depression as a gestalt

Depression, too, is a whole of behaviour, patterns, ways of processing information, a true gestalt. All kinds of explanations are given for the behaviour of a depressed person and solutions offered to all the explainable parts of the whole. Effectively responding to some of these parts can certainly be beneficial. The simple sum of all parts, however, can eventually only in dribs and drabs explain that someone does not get any joy anymore out of life as a whole. So little joy in some cases, that it seems better to leave life.

'The internal world of a depressed person is different from that of a non-depressed person.'

Depression is a gestalt state. And only by analysing how these complex states of mind arise can we find answers on how to change this experience. By examining how our gestalt is built up, we can find answers to those states of mind that have the greatest impact on our lives, the life choices we make or just fail to make. For, not only our impeding states, such as depression, are gestalt states but also our most beautiful states are compound states of mind.

Which are common factors of a depressed mindset?[37]

- You experience your situation as hopeless.
- Things in general and life feel pointless.
- It's dark.
- You feel empty.
- You have the feeling of being in a vacuum.
- You feel despondent.
- You have thoughts of doom.
- You feel listless.
- It is a matter of tunnel vision.
- You think you are pathetic and experience self-pity.
- You feel your paralyzed.
- You feel alone and feel like you have to face life alone.
- You feel a victim.

37 This list of experiences and states is composed of interviews with clients and trainees from my training courses (over a period of ten years) who have at some time been dejected or depressed in their lives.

- Your perception is distorted: small things become bigger, fear worsens, you make things personal.
- You often don't like others, not to be trusted, you can even hate others.
- You may feel betrayed by others.
- You believe that most people are bad.
- You have the feeling that 'it' happens or things happen to you.
- You have no goals because you don't see your future.

You are different

The internal world of a depressed person is different from that of a non-depressed person. That makes friends and loved ones feel so often powerless. 'Nothing seems to affect Peter,' says his caring wife. 'Whatever I do or say, I keep getting a kind of blank answer; I begin to feel despondent due to this.' Simply setting goals, finding meaning, undertaking activities may be meaningful actions but we do not know for sure. Any intervention, technique, stimulating activity is actually *a stab in the dark*, a gamble: when you get going with someone on the off-chance, assuming that the inner landscape of the person matches your world, the world of a non-depressed person. However, this is fundamentally incorrect. The inner landscape of a depressed person is different from that of a non-depressed person. When you think about it, it is crucial to realize that depression is a gestalt state. How can we change or influence the 'molecule' if we do not understand that it is the precise composition of reference frameworks, beliefs, conclusions in combination with the lack of a way out (goal), which ultimately causes you to stop moving completely?

As with any careful chemical experiment, precision is required as to what elements together make up the molecule. And not only what elements are used, but certainly also their quantitative proportions, cooking time, cooling-off time and so on. If the experiment has been successful, the gases have become water. The depression molecule is also an accurately devised molecule. Setbacks, loneliness and an altered self-image, will ensure in time that past experiences get a new meaning. Beliefs that you have about yourself and others can change. Pessimistic thoughts and character traits can strengthen the process. Expectations not coming true change your future perspective and view on the past. Feelings of helplessness and powerlessness are increasingly being stirred up until the moment you stop taking initiative at all. Then something inside has changed. Then something has changed in your inner world, and the only thing we see on the outside is dejection.

Summary

Depression is a gestalt, a seemingly inexplicable phenomenon if you only look at it from the independent parts, the symptoms. When you realize that a depression gestalt arises by bringing together a number of unique thoughts and feelings, the depression that in this way arises is much better understood. The unique composition of these thoughts and feelings makes your inner world change, making you feel misunderstood and alone. Moreover, you don't know what is going on inside you, you just feel different. This feeling is reinforced owing to the fact that the outside world is approaching you from out of a totally different world. Depression is difficult to understand for yourself and your environment. Therefore, in the next chapter, we go one step further to explore the depression landscape together.

11.
Dark landscape

One of the things that particularly surprised me when I was depressed myself (and didn't yet know it at the time) is that I didn't do anything about it. I felt rotten, everything was meaningless, I didn't experience a connection anymore and I didn't recognize myself anymore... and I didn't do a thing! As I described in the introduction of this book: Months passed and I did nothing! I didn't understand, but those thoughts were no reason at all to develop any initiative whatsoever to help myself. I was aware of it, did not understand, but nevertheless didn't do a thing. I sometimes told others and the few people I still spoke to, did their utmost to help and inspire me, but nothing affected me. I heard them but had no feeling anymore about things like 'Let's do something nice', 'Cheer up, tomorrow things will be looking up again.' Despite the well-intentioned remarks, I had no connection with them. As a fact, I understood everyone very well, because I knew that what they were telling me existed in the world, but it didn't exist in *me* anymore! In me all the beautiful things they were talking about had vanished, as if I had ended up in a total void. A weird experience, when people talk about beautiful things, that you know there can be beautiful things outside of you, but that you don't feel any interest to get to know these beautiful things, or to receive in your life or to be able to feel. It is there for others, but no longer for you and that's what it is, there is nothing you can do about it. That is the final state of mind that you get into, you have to make do with it.

The problem with depression is that people continue to focus on the things that were once present in the world 'outside', without realizing how their inner world has changed. In this chapter *Dark landscape* I take you to the inner perspective of depression. I show that the inner world of a depressed person is dark and closed. This is meant literally. I explain that depression is a kind of mental infarct where you lose all your landmarks. You will discover that there is a real distinction between 'inside' and 'outside' and that by listening to what a depressed person tells you, you can discover how the inner landscape of depression looks. A depressed person in fact tells you exactly where he or she is!

Two Worlds

It is a strange phenomenon, the difference between observing the outside world and the perception that takes place from our inside world. For many people, this is a frightening concept.

INNER MIRROR IMAGE

'Do you mean that my mindset determines how I see things? I find this a scary idea', says trainee Jaap. 'For that would mean that nothing is real, right?'

'Well, it's not quite like that. We represent the world around us. Our brain creates, as it were, an inner mirror image of what we perceive in the world. That inner mirror image is in its turn coloured by our experiences and memories. The fusion of what can be perceived in the world outside of us with our experiences and memories makes us interpret things the way we do. So we are, as it were, responding to our interpretation of the world and not so much to the world itself. Our interpretation of the world around us is based on a unique landscape.'

'Do you mean that all my thoughts and feelings, all my beliefs and the ideas I have about something happening in my life create a kind of filter between me and the world around me?'

'You could put it like that. See it as a kind of curtain that you look through and that influences your perception, and if

you were to take a little step back you would discover an inner landscape.'
'Like in the movie The Matrix?'
'Yes, that's about it.'

'A depressed person is not negative, he just doesn't see it. Actually a depressed person tells exactly what he is living in.'

A completely dark room

The composition of the depression gestalt does something special inside: The inner world of the person becomes dark. I mean this literally. The inner landscape becomes foggy, colourless, drab, grey, and even pitch dark. This is expressed first and foremost in the person's language. 'Everything is drab and grey', 'I don't see a way out', 'For me it's colourless', 'I see no light at the end of the tunnel', 'I'm looking for a ray of hope.' Gradually it begins to express itself in the person's behaviour. Moving less and less, becoming more and more passive and withdrawing from social situations. Even if everyone calls out how much fun it is outside, you don't have a connection with it. The depression molecule slowly locks you up in a darkening room. What happens outside that room becomes less and less meaningful and thus your loneliness becomes bigger and bigger.

The depression molecule has created a very special inner landscape. Namely, a *completely dark room* which no trace of light enters any more. It is so dark that the realization of what is 'outside the room' has vanished. There is such an emphatic darkness that the person in the room no longer moves, for, after all, there is no reason to move.

'Fifty percent of your experience takes place inside.'

The person in question him- or herself doesn't know that he or she lives in a completely dark room, but is aware of two overlapping images, that of the outside world and that of his or her inside world. The only features of this state of mind are that the person talks about things like 'dark moods', 'dark clouds', 'dark humour', 'everything is grey and drab' and so on. Therefore, a depressed person can look at something beautiful outside and only speak about darkness, meaninglessness and distance. Looked at it this way, the depressed person is not negative, he just doesn't perceive it. Actually a depressed person tells exactly what world he or she lives in.

Signals from a dark (inner) landscape

- You are not able to experience any or scarcely any happiness at all.
- You feel gloomy, sad, down, dejected.
- Words like 'nice', 'pleasant', 'enjoy', 'fun', have no or less meaning.
- You feel alone in the world in spite of the presence of others.
- You don't succeed in escaping your situation on your own.
- You don't see any reason to get out of your situation (because you do not know why). You lack Initiative, every impetus for initiative has evaporated.
- You lack a sense of later, tomorrow and the day after tomorrow.
- You believe there is no one for you.
- You believe that no one loves you.
- You have the feeling that you are stuck in darkness without an idea of a way out.
- You feel passive and take no initiative to change your situation, and if there is any initiative at all, it is about other matters, things of the moment.

- You do want something, but don't take any steps yourself.
- You don't want to live any longer.

Mental infarct

If you are depressed, an emphatic break comes to pass between the inside and outside world, you don't perceive a link anymore with things that you used to get a vibe off, and 'doing fun things' has become pointless. The world outside your world seems to have disappeared, though you do see and know that the world 'beyond' is just there. All these phenomena I know from the time I worked as a physiotherapist with people with brain injuries in an academic rehabilitation clinic in London. From the many drastic experiences in that hospital one experience has kept stuck in my brain. It illustrates how our mind-body-emotion system works. With most strokes, parts of the body fail and, depending on where the brain lesion is, arms, legs and parts of the face may get spastically paralyzed or someone's speech fails, for example.[38] Cognitive changes often take place like, for instance, a poor capability of estimating distance, time or space. Very awkward problems, since this kind of orientation functions are built

38 CerebroVascular Accident (CVA), or stroke

deep in our *hardware*, in order to be able to function in the world from that base. If, just like a small child, you cannot estimate how deep a stairwell is, or how far away the water in a canal is, then functioning freely can be very tricky and even frightening.

In addition to these functions, which are often hampered or even lost, there is still another. Our brain takes care of the representation of our body. In other words, our body exists in our brain and in our body we feel that. An example: One day a lady was brought into the ward with acute brain injury. After a first diagnosis, she was laid apart for further research. The next morning, she woke up screaming. The medical staff hurried to her room. In the room we found the woman in great panic. Holding her left forearm with her right hand, she shouted: 'There is a stranger in my bed!' She was fully convinced that the left arm she held in her hand was not hers, but a stranger's. The brain part that had stored her left body half in her brain was so damaged that the *software* that recognized her left body half no longer functioned. Because the hardware that made the software work had broken, she recognized her body no longer as part of herself. Why? It no longer existed in her own brain. So, although her left body half was still present and healthy, she assessed that part of her body as strange, not belonging her.

In a way, the symptoms of such a cerebral infarct resemble what a depressive gestalt eventually creates in the inner landscape of a depressed person, but without brain damage. You understand that there is an 'outside'. A world outside that dark inner world. However, that world 'beyond' has disappeared. In your inner landscape, the world outside doesn't exist anymore. In this sense, you can compare the phenomenon of depression with a stroke, but then as a kind of *mental* infarct. Our brain represents the world for us, so we know that there is a world for us to participate in and take action in. Because of the depressive gestalt this understanding disappears, and so do other things like 'soon' and 'the future'...[39]

Looked at in this way, the final result of the precise composition of the depression molecule is quite drastic. Just imagine what it would be like not to have an inner awareness of 'beyond', 'later' and 'the future', and that, besides, words like 'nice', 'fun', 'happiness' have lost their meaning and you don't find your interests captivating any more. That you are all alone and that the things you usually do go wrong, reinforcing the feeling that you had better stay inside...

In the Darkness

Lock yourself up in a room without windows, turn off the light in the corridor, leave your mobile outside the room. It is fairly difficult to completely cut off yourself from light; find a place where that is possible. Turn off all phones, make sure there's no trace of light coming in anymore, nothing, nothing at all. Then turn around three times so you don't remember where the entrance is. If you don't have a real room or can't find one, imagine it. Imagine then having been placed here and have no landmarks left. Imagine that there's nothing outside the room you're in...

Listen with attention

How do you get out of a dark room that you don't know you're in and don't know how you got there? That seems like an almost impossible task. Once you begin to realize that you are inhabiting your own unique landscape, you are going to listen better to people and yourself. When you

---

39 It is beyond the purpose of this book to discuss all elements of the depressive gestalt. These are discussed in depth in the depression and zest for life coach training and during the two day depression and zest for live Masterclass. See Wassilizafiris.nl.

start listening with attention you hear that people describe their inner landscape to you.

In an interview in which actor and singer Antonie Kamerling[40] was asked about his life, family and depression, Antonie made some remarkable statements about his inner landscape.

FLIPPING THE SWITCH

I: You've said some time in the past: 'I feel the duty to be happy.'
AK: 'On average I've been happy in the last few months. Before, I wasn't. A few months ago, I was depressed as usual, and I was utterly fed up with it. I was so angry, just because I have everything, I have everything to be happy. Isa (his wife, ed.) has been yelling for years: 'You have to flip the switch.' Apparently, she can do that. I could never find that switch. A switch in yourself. I also used to take it very seriously, I thought: 'Oh, I'll never ever get out of this. I was very passive in my depression. If it were to come again, I'd be looking for that switch again. I don't know exactly where it is, it had to do with some kind of anger, I just don't want this.'

I: 'What was it you wanted?'
AK: 'I just wanted to live. It's like you're alive dead, it also takes so long, sometimes it takes a week, but it feels like a year. You only feel grey, even when your children are sitting in front of you, your wife, your career. If you haven't had it for so long, you're extra happy to be happy. Very often I don't want to go to bed. I haven't done things for years because I was too shiftless. So, I really still want this and that...'

In the above interview, Antonie Kamerling gives quite a lot of information about his inner world. One of the striking

40 Antonie Kamerling suffered from bipolar disorder and ended his life on October 6, 2010. He was interviewed by Klaas Drupsteen for the NCRV programme *Het Hoogste Woord* (*Hogging the Limelight*) on December 26, 2007.

things is that he could 'never find that switch', while 'Isa has been yelling that for years'. 'I don't know where it is'. He says he thought he would never come out of it again and in one and the same breath he says how passive he was in his depression. 'It is as if you were alive dead.' His sense of time had also changed 'as if it lasted a year, while it was only a week'. Kamerling tells that he 'only felt grey', even when his most important loved ones were sitting in front of him.

And with the question 'What, indeed, did you want?' comes the greatest desire: 'I just wanted to live.' That ultimate desire seems to be a very ordinary wish, but in his inner landscape 'just live' did not exist. The problem with depression is that people continue to focus on the things that were once present in the world 'outside', without realizing how their inner world has changed.

Metaphorical landscape

At least fifty percent of our experiences take place within us. That this is so literal you might not have imagined. Our brain creates a logical and a more metaphorical world; a landscape in which we move, where there is space and quarters of the compass, colours and shades of grey, passageways and obstructions. In this internal landscape, real world affairs are represented, such as: houses, mountains, seas, forests, cars and so on, but unlike our real world these elements do not necessarily have the same meaning. The elements of our inner landscape are more metaphorical, meaning they refer to experiences we have and not necessarily to the meaning as we know it in the outside world. My research shows that when, for example, you have a problem with someone and do not make any progress, whatever you try, you may walk, in the proverbial sense, up against a wall. This people can also say literally. It is my perception that in this case there is a great chance that in your inner landscape you will have a wall in front of you. What you are telling is something you already knew (in this case), namely that you are not making any headway (with the person concerned). Your subconscious mind has recreated that experience in a metaphorical sense because a wall you run into clearly represents what you are experiencing. Andrew Austin has made a similar discovery. In his *Metaphors of Movement-method*[41], he has you discover in a special way how you can explore and transform your inner landscape.

The metaphorical landscape of depression is empty, dark and obstructed, cut off from the logical world outside us. The only features of that landscape are the words you use when feeling depressed and the inner experience that only you go through. You may be in a pit or an enclosed space or even floating in the infinity of the universe. The obstacles are the same: you are alone, have no influence, it is dark or gloomy and you are closed off from the world beyond your landscape. In Part 3, *ZEST FOR LIFE*, I take you along to how to make your inner landscape even more visible. By using a few crucial exercises, you learn to transform your inner landscape. Your inner perception can then change into a sense of connection rather than being shut off, together instead of alone and the feeling of having influence rather than being helpless or hopeless. But it all starts with a trace of light in your dark landscape.

41 See: www.metaphorsofmovement.co.uk

Summary

There is a difference between 'inside' and 'outside'. The depressed gestalt creates a different inner landscape: a dark world that is separated from the world beyond that landscape. In a literal sense, you no longer move because you have no reason to move when you feel depressed. The bizarre thing about all this is that you are not consciously aware of this yourself, but all the same experience it within. You can compare depression to a mental infarct where the world outside your dark world seems to have disappeared, as if you were cut off. Also, it is not a coincidence that you have lost your interest in the beautiful things of life because, inside, the outside world has disappeared, and hence the future. By listening you can hear how someone describes his or her landscape. These are metaphorical references that are clues to that inner landscape. In our inner landscape the same natural laws are in force as outside, only our experiences are metaphorically represented. These representations give us important information about what you are experiencing inside. In the final chapter of this section, happiness and depression come together and I will answer the questions raised by the fourth and fifth assumptions of DSM thinking (Chapter 8): What is your goal when you feel depressed? And what happiness can we strive for to open the depression landscape so that light can shine in your darkness.

12.
The happiness lessons of gloom

We all know that the pressure exerted by an achievement-oriented society may contribute to depressive feelings. Performance pressure is one of the manifestations of life in a world where being happy has become our ultimate endeavour. In the last chapter of this section we look again at the way we think about happiness as described in the first part. For convenience, I call it 'happinessthink.' This happinessthink we are going to link to what we now know about depression. Our happinessthink is so intertwined with our language use that we do not realize the impact of this on the emergence and strengthening of depressive feelings. Dejection is not just nasty and annoying. When you view the world from the depressive landscape, you can discover important clues about how to open the door to lasting happiness.

To help you set that door ajar in your dark landscape, I will discuss in this chapter the three main principles that make the difference: **1. Where are you?** Start from where you are in the depressive landscape, otherwise you are trying to achieve something that simply does not exist in your world; **2. From being happy to 'having luck'.** Define 'happiness' correctly, because only in that way you know what you are looking for in your daily life; **3. The opposite of depression**. Define the opposite of depression, because then you can learn to work in the long run on a lasting form of happiness in your life.

The difference between wanting and being

'I just want to be happy,' says the umpteenth person when I ask the question 'What do you want?'

Depressive people are eminently good at setting great, unachievable goals, projected on a vanished future. It is curious to realize that we are conditioned by our happinessthink and so set wrong targets. The nasty thing is that we are often unaware of what the impact is of the things we want and desire.

> 'You have everything necessary to build something that is larger than yourself.'
>
> *Seth Godin*

Happinessthink has its roots in the idea that everything is possible, and that our most important assets are willpower and the belief that it is within each individual's power to make himself into what he or she wants. We are taught that we can accomplish anything by simply wanting it and that we can achieve anything if only we try hard enough. Yet, there are limitations attending this thought, though in many cases it is true that we can do more than we think we can. Mark Fisher remarks about this in *The politics of depression* [42] that this thought also causes despair, which is to be blamed on the illusion that everything is achievable for us if only we want to. The simple fact that we don't as easily get a promotion as desired and don't simply earn more just by wanting it and don't have a nice relationship just like that, will make you feel more helpless, because deep inside you feel that not everything you want is

---

42 Anindya Bhattacharyya, *The politics of depression: Mark Fisher on mental health and class confidence*, rs21, www.rs21.org.uk, 27 april, 2014

within reach.[43] As time passes, your feelings change into powerlessness and in a deep sense of having no influence, says Fisher. We know that not everything is granted us, but all the same we long for it. The gap between where we are and where we want to be is so great that it strengthens our powerlessness and ultimately paralyzes us with the idea that it is not in store for us.

The conviction that our will makes it possible for us to achieve everything and the associated failure that this may eventually entail, also confirms that if you do not succeed, you yourself are responsible for your failure. Obviously, you don't deserve to have that ultimate happiness. Depression is then a *self-fulfilling prophecy*, in which feelings of worthlessness, uselessness and 'it is surely not in store for me' materialize due to the depressed person's total passivity.

> 'What is more interesting to pursue is the experience of luck: to have luck and the feeling of prosperity which this entails.'

1. Where are you?

It is crucial to realize that you can only 'leave' for some form of happiness if you know where you are. In the context of depression, it is therefore very important to realize that if you live in 'a dark room' what you want to achieve is related to that room. Dreaming about things that lie outside this room without knowing how to get out of it will only bring disappointment. You skip a step in your thinking: you are in the dark room and would like to exert influence; this is only possible if your goals are in this dark room.

43 Roy Baumeister, *Willpower – Rediscovering the greatest Human Strength*, 2011

2. From being happy to having luck

To pursue happiness without being specific is one of the problems of our pursuit of happiness. We create grand, nonspecific ideas about happiness and all these grand nonspecific matters are far beyond our inner landscape. Yes, we do know they exist in the world: beautiful cars, houses, great careers, charming partners, eternal youth and loving children... but in 'our room' they do not exist. People with clinical forms of depression are more inclined to set abstract targets that are difficult to reach. 'I want to be happy' turns out to be one of the commonest goals (unlike, for example, a specific goal like 'I want to run five kilometres in X time'). This is also confirmed by Dr. Joanne Dickson in her research.[44] In addition, it appears that depressed persons put forward nonspecific reasons ('I couldn't help it' instead of 'I got up half an hour late for the appointment') for whether or not achieving their happiness targets.

A consequence of the pursuit of these grand desires is that the goals are unattainable, which strengthens the feeling of depression. This creates a downward spiral of negative thoughts.

Consequently, the grand desire 'wanting to be happy' is very difficult to visualize. Especially when, being depressed, you are longing for a happy life because the enclosed dark room makes visualizing (however specific) a useless activity. In your inner landscape the room is dark, gloomy and closed off. No matter how hard you do your best, you won't get out of it and you know it. It appears from my research that you can only make the next step if you see a bright spot. For this to happen the door has to be ajar first. Before that time, visualizing is useless. Worse still, dreaming of a happy life confirms and strengthens the solitary confinement that you are condemned to. This moving back and forth between desire on the one hand

---

44 Joanne Dickson, *People with depression tend to pursue generalized goals*, University of Liverpool, Institute of Psychology - University News, 8 July 2013

and inner reality on the other hand strengthens and deepens your personal feelings of failure, inability and discouragement. So, it is terribly important to be specific in the dark room instead of setting vague, grand and general targets, which are outside of your room.

The right name of happiness

As in Part 1 *HAPPINESS* has already become clear, it is a lot more interesting to pursue 'having luck' rather than 'being happy'. The feeling of prosperity that comes from this experience of happiness makes you feel that things can come your way. Being lucky is a core part of the happy life we so desire. In the part *ZEST FOR LIFE*, I enter at length into it.

'Happiness is not the opposite of depression.'

3. The opposite of depression

It is essential to know what the ultimate gestalt is you want to work on if you want lasting happiness in your life. As I have described before, there is no purpose if you are depressed. Nowhere is described what you are aiming for then, and that is not a trifle. The fact is, happiness is not simply the opposite of depression. But what, then, is the opposite of depression? To arrive somewhere it is just as important to know where you are as to know where you want to go. Although it is not clear what you should strive for when you are depressed, it is necessary to find out what that ultimate state of mind is. For, when you have deconstructed the depression gestalt, you need direction (your desired state of mind) so that you can collect the elements that will help you create this desired state of mind.

In my research on depression I have asked many hundreds of people (students and clients, over a period of ten years): 'Please, describe the opposite of being depressed.' Everyone then described his or her experience, but no one the opposite state of mind of depression. See in the frame *The opposite of being depressed* a selection of these descriptions.

The opposite of being depressed

- You have a future perspective.
- You have the belief that it is going to be right.
- The experiences you have, and even life, are perceived as meaningful and significant.
- You see a bright spot.
- You see 'a way out.'
- Your perspective is wider.
- You're oriented outward.
- You can see everything through 'rose-coloured glasses'.
- You have an overview.
- You experience light and feel light.
- You think in 'in-between colours'.
- You have a good feeling.
- You can put into perspective.
- You have humour and can laugh.
- You're energetic.
- You experience self-esteem.
- You feel powerful and feel you can have influence.
- You give 'active' meaning and feel: I can do something about it.
- You feel together.
- You have faith in others and you believe that most people are nice.
- You feel safe.
- You feel optimistic.
- You're elated.

- You're playful.
- You are open.
- You are active.
- You think creatively.
- You feel physically relaxed and mentally clear.
- You can muster the courage for tough challenges.
- You are enterprising.
- You experience a sense of pleasure and have a 'broad' mind to do things.
- You're experiencing happiness.
- You are happy about your joy.

A new gestalt

Imagine that you would experience all these states of mind as described in the frame. Imagine you feel as described here. What state arises when you experience all the above-mentioned feelings, beliefs, thoughts and ideas? Even though you're experiencing it only for a moment: What gestalt awakens in you when you experience, feel, sincerely think, believe all the above, and have integrated into your being and life?

'For a depressed person luck is very close'

Then you experience zest for life!

This is an odd state because *zest for life is simply embracing life and the desire to live and go on living.* And the desire to continue living is perhaps the most important counterpart of depression.

'Whoever misses this vitality (life force) may be heading for a premature funeral.'

Henri Bergson

Zest for life is linked to two related states of mind: 'joy of living' and 'life force'.

Joy of living (French: joie de vivre) amounts to delight, pleasure in life, and life force[45] is the vital force necessary for the evolution and development of an organism. These three gestalts have a lot of affinity and describe all three of them very complex emotional states. Why complex? Because you cannot create them just like that. I mean, they are complex because they consist of multiple components, there is not one single factor that leads to one of these states of mind, there are several factors that make it possible for zest for life to arise.

If zest for life were to exist just like that, all those books about becoming happy would not be needed at all, then we just pulled it out of the cupboard and voilà, there you have zest for life. And sometimes, sometimes we succeed, and we feel it again, that zest for life. But what did we do then? What miracle have we made possible in ourselves? Which seemingly unrelated elements have been brought together to create that miraculous new thing, that which did not yet exist and which you have been looking for so long? Which elements need to be brought together to stir up that new state so that zest for life is awakened, so that life becomes a treat again, a delight? In the subsequent part, I take you step by step along in how to build and activate this cheerful state of mind...

45 Wikipedia: Élan vital

'Zest for life is the opposite of depression.'

Summary

By viewing the world from the dejected perspective, we get important clues about what happiness actually is, how our longing for happiness can make us depressed and in what manner we should think to find that sort of happiness that makes us flourish. Dejection teaches us that we have to set the right targets. For if you have unachievable desires, slowly but surely feelings of powerlessness and lack of influence emerge. But it's not just the right goals that matter. Dejection also tells us where the domain of our goals is, namely very close by, in your inner landscape. Right on the spot where you are, right now, in the dark. Because only then you discover what you need to work on. Do not even desire things that are in the light, the abstract desires that are out of your reach, because they strengthen your dejection. Stop 'wanting to be happy', this is the basis of your problem, because it actually makes you miserable. Realize that 'having luck' is an energizing state of mind and that it opens a road to your future. All these things together help you find the glimmer of light that is needed in your dark landscape. In the end, depression teaches us that we should not only go on describing the problem, but, on the contrary, the opposite: zest for life. When you know what you can build up, it is possible to run down and dismantle dejection. In the subsequent part *ZEST FOR LIFE* that is exactly what we are going to do.

Light at the
end of the
tunnel

Zest for life

Introduction part 3
Zest for life

When I became aware of the fact that an opposite state
of mind is needed to get out of dejection, my own voyage
of discovery began. For, although I had no idea how I
could feel high-spirited, this changed my perception. My
clients confirmed this. It didn't all of a sudden change
the darkness they experienced, but the perception of this
darkness did change. You can compare it with packing
your suitcase for a trip. If you don't know where you are
going, packing your suitcase is tricky, because it may be
cold or, on the contrary, very hot at the destination. Maybe
walking shoes are convenient to carry with you, or just
flip-flops. If you don't know where you're going, you would
really want to take everything with you to make sure you've
got what you need at your destination. Once you know
where your journey is going, your attitude changes. You
will pack selectively and the choices you make are clear.
You can then prepare yourself perfectly for your trip.
And your preparation starts at the place where you are, at
home. I and my clients experienced just that. By realizing
what your actual destination is, the place where you are
becomes more visible. When you have a clearer vision of
where you are, it becomes much more obvious what your
first steps ought to be.

Knowing where you want to go, doesn't cause you to know
how to get there. How do you shift a depressed gestalt into
a spirited one? The ingredients have all been dealt with
before in this book. I have talked about the three triggers
for depression:

1. loneliness
2. (abruptly) changing self-image
3. (chronic) adversity

The combination of two or more of these elements doesn't
so much change the world around us as the world in us.

People give off subtle, but clear clues about the world they inhabit. And although every human being is unique and has his or her own inner experience, the composition of the depression gestalt causes the inner landscape of a depressed person to become dark. So dark that the person doesn't see a way out at any given moment. Not because there are no ways out, but because the person's world no longer gives permission to see them. Evidently, the feeling of being on your own, unwanted, not belonging and not being up to scratch in a world that is against you, is enough to want to stay out of that world. In the human psyche, a dark space is an excellent place to hide.

In order to create zest for life it is essential to dismantle the depressive gestalt. By examining the landscape, you will get clues about what to change. In deconstructing this depressive gestalt and letting a new one emerge; it is not enough to change one element. It is the unique confluence of multiple qualities that change your internal world. All these facets together ensure that the door can be ajar again, or, as a client said to me the other day: 'It's like there are all kinds of bright spots coming through the wall.' In the final part of *Happiness is Depressing, ZEST FOR LIFE*, I take you step by step along the most important elements necessary to change your internal landscape. Evoking crucial states of mind, like acknowledgement, self-acceptance, ownership, optimism and ultimately luck, not only opens the door, but simultaneously opens a new gestalt: zest for life, the desire to live.

We can only dismantle the old if we understand that our current inner experience has not only been created by a series of life experiences, but also because our way of thinking about matters like being happy, being lucky, depression and zest for life. For our way of thinking about these matters has shaped our inner and outer world. The flawed assumptions we make about this are the basis of our thinking and therefore our actions. New descriptions of what happiness is, and a clearer picture of what depression is, are key elements to develop new models, which are better attuned to the human experience. And it is that human experience where the secrets of our development are waiting for us.

In chapters 13 and 14 you'll discover more about your inner landscape. This is important because you want to get to know your point of departure. I explain how your personal interpretation of an experience determines whether that experience becomes meaningful or meaningless and how that makes your landscape lighter or darker. I have already said that our happinessthink virtually forces us to look outside, whereas you will only get to know your landscape by looking inside. In the chapters from 15 onwards you will build up zest for life step by step. In Chapter 15 you will learn how to transform feelings of loneliness, of being misunderstood and forsaken. *Dealing with loneliness* teaches you what the basis is of being emotionally connected, and not on your own. The perception that there are people around you, that you feel connected and even supported, is an essential element of zest for life. You will find that this will give you a boost and trust to continue.

In Chapter 16 *I'm OK* I explain why a stable self-image is important for us and how to update a changed self-image so that you can feel whole and self-satisfied once more. In addition, you are steered towards ideas that help you to feel valued by others, so that you realize that you are precious in the eyes of others. A healthy, stable and, above all, truthful self-image helps you to live in peace with yourself and to pave the way for zest for life. In *From Adversity to Prosperity* (Chapter 17) you lay an important foundation for the-zest-for-life gestalt. In this chapter you will discover what you can influence. Instead of yearning for solutions beyond your landscape, you'll experience how it feels to affect the landscape where you are. This sense of influence is directly the basis of your ability to transform your pessimistic thinking style into an optimistic way of thinking. These crucial aspects will prepare you for what will come in Chapter 18, *Good-luck magnet*. There you learn what happiness really is and how 'luck' can open your perspective to the outside world and the future. All these aspects together make it possible that light can shine in your landscape and this light is the foundation of your zest for life. In Chapter 18 you can then explore your own (new) landscape, so you will be able to have a clear vision of it in the weeks and months to come. *Happiness is Depressing* ends with the chapter *Universal motives.* In Chapter 19, we connect your natural motives to goals and desires. This creates perspective, which is the last building block of zest for life: the appetite for life and the desire to go on with life.

Finally, I take you along to how my personal story of transformation progressed and I offer you some ideas to have your new landscape fertile in the future, too. Are you ready?

An appetite
for life and
the desire to
go on living

13.
A different relation to problems

To take you along to an animated gestalt, it is important to do something paradoxical first: forget where you want to go. I have already discussed in several ways that our quest for happiness is an important part of dejection and unhappiness. The first step is to discover where you are and then claim and own where you are. Not only do we want to dish up our lives more beautifully than they are, we also want to dish up ourselves more beautifully than we are. Unfortunately, this strategy is only effective for a short time. If you don't address the bigger problem you're having, you'll continue to look for workarounds and your problem will slowly but surely increase or you will live a life with (big) ups and downs. In order to transform the real problem you need to get to know the problem better. Which means that you need to explore where you are instead of determining straight away where you want to go. I understand that this may be an uncomfortable thought for you. However, it needn't be, because a problem is the issue that needs to be resolved[46], and that is exactly what it is. Our inner landscape is created by, among other things, meaning. In this chapter I will delve deeper into the influence of meaningfulness and meaninglessness on your landscapes. I will take you to your problem so that you know exactly which issue needs to be resolved in order to take off.

---

46 The Oxford Dictionary of English Etymology, and several online dictionaries

> 'I just want to be happy:
> I want to be, as a matter of
> course, in a constant pleasant
> state of contentment.'

Doomed wish for happiness

Our pursuit of a happy life may have a nasty aftertaste. Happiness seems to be our enlightenment. In our desire for the light, we have developed an inability to look back and see how long our own shadow has become. We have developed an inability to see where we are. We are stuck in two ways. On the one hand we strive for great and often unachievable goals, and on the other hand we often have a very limited insight into where we are.

In the minds of (depressed) people we find the (opportunistic) need to want 'grand' and 'far'. As if that were the most natural thing in the world. 'I just want to be happy' is actually 'I want to be, as a matter of course, in a constant pleasant state of contentment'. As if *that* is a natural state that we should permanently stay in. It is extremely important to realize that this is a state of mind that is impossible and even undesirable. For this reason alone, our subconscious mind has good cause to oppose it.

Being happy is for us an end station and that end station ought to be straight away the start of... uhm... what again? The starting point of our trip? For, when we have arrived at that place where we are in that pleasant state of contentment, then... what was it again? Then it starts! Doesn't it? The desire for that paradise is so great that we have exalted this vague state of mind over all others. For the sake of convenience, we forget that we don't know exactly what that pleasant state is, and because we have no or little insight into where we are, we have no idea where to start. The consequences are easy to predict: an, as time passes, increasing feeling of disappointment and additional evidence for the proof that happiness isn't, in one way or another, for you.

This pursuit of happiness is a doomed endeavour. Doomed, because we, and even less a miserable person, will never arrive at that place where time stands still in perpetual enlightenment.

GERARD

Wishes for happiness occur in all kinds of forms, but the general characteristic is the infeasibility of the desire uttered. Gerard told me during one of our conversations that he can feel so tense when he is with other people.

'I would like to feel equal to other people. Well, no, that's wrong, I want to feel important, head and shoulders above others.'

'Are you actually saying that you feel less, smaller than others?'

'Yes, that's right.'

'So, if I understand correctly, you are the smallest in your landscape, and you would like to be bigger than the people outside your landscape? And you feel tense all the time when you are with other people?'

'Yes, that's right.'

'Gerard, I think it's not so strange that you have been feeling so tense near other people for years. You yearn for something that is not in store for you. You want to be bigger than others, but how on earth could you make this happen?'

As long as Gerard could remember 'being important' was number one on his wish list, but, not realizing that in his inner landscape he could never become bigger than others, he continued to pursue something that in the end only got him one thing: a chronic tension and the increasingly prominent sense that he is inferior to other people. The glorification of 'being important' is his pursuit of 'being happy'.

> ‘Someone who thinks
> things go smoothly, is in
> for many problems.’
>
> *Lao-Tse*

As soon as possible

Our happinessthink makes us want to solve our problems
as quickly as possible. In the external world (the tangible
world we live in) this is sometimes very useful. Suppose
there is a fallen tree in front of your door and you want
to enter your house. Then it is convenient to grab a saw
as soon as possible and make a passage so you can enjoy
a delicious cup of coffee inside. This is different in our
inner world. If there is a proverbial fallen tree between
you and your pursuit of happiness, what are you going to
do? Are you going to saw the tree down? How then? What
will actually happen when you saw the tree down? Why is
that tree there? Has there been a storm? Did I come by
the wrong path? Where have I come from and where am
I actually going? These and many more questions apply to
our internal landscape. We are in an awkward predicament
because the ‘solution’ appeals to us, but our solutions are
simply bad if we do not know what we are solving.

ANNA

*In a coaching session, Anna told me that she always says things
her partner gets angry about. Before I could ask a question, she
told me that the solution is simple.*
‘I just have to restrain myself in conversations with my friend.’
Simple. A problem and, yes, a solution. Would you think?
*‘Why are you coming to me if you know that this is the solution
to your problem?’*
‘Well, actually I don’t really know, it’s also such a fuss.’
‘Fuss?’
*‘Yes, he is hypersensitive, touchy and I can never do things
right.’*

'O, you don't have a problem, but he has?'
'Well, if I just learn to count up to ten it's solved.'
'You've had this problem... how long?'
'Well, I've been doing this all along, only for me it's just
chatting away cosily, but what I say always disturbs him so.'
'So, your problem is that you have an over-sensitive husband?'
'Ha ha, yes, it certainly looks like that. I myself don't think
it's much of a problem, either, but he...' 'It's pretty interesting,
though, that you don't think it's such a problem that your friend
bickers with you every day about the fact that you obviously
blurt out all kinds of things he's disturbed by.'
Silence.
'What's your problem then, Anna?'
Anna's 'solutions' are no solutions for the simple reason that
she knows too little about the problem she is in the middle of. It
seems like a reflex that is in us to immediately devise a half-
baked solution. Without realizing that we don't know the essence
of the problem and therefore cannot arrive at a real solution.

Solving is inextricably linked to happiness. 'Effective', 'successful', 'S.M.A.R.T.' (the latter is a method of setting goals which stands for: Specific, Measurable, Acceptable, Realistic, Temporal) all come from the unsatisfiable need for happiness and everything beautiful. The issue is often not resolved simply because it is too uncomfortable for us to face the real problem.

Not knowing what you *do* have

In determining depression-like phenomena the DSM is used as a reference. If you show a few symptoms from it, you are soon to be classified as depressed. The doctor or practitioner makes this diagnosis using the general guidelines of the DSM symptoms list on depression. Then nothing is known yet about the person's inner experience. What do you actually know when you say: 'I haven't been feeling happy for a while?' Actually, only something about the state you are not in, namely being happy. We don't know anything about the state you are in. We know nothing about what thoughts and feelings you do have, what assessment you make, what emotions you experience: We don't know anything about your inner landscape.

Our inner experience and the world around us can differ and often do so. As has been discussed in the second part of this book *DEPRESSION*: That inner world, we look through it as it were. Our inner world could be seen as a veil you filter the world with, not only regarding how information comes in but also how you view the outside world. The problem? We are not aware of that veil. Our senses are focused on the outside world, so our focus is not on the world behind the veil.

As a gloomy person, you are usually not aware that your inner landscape is changing. You really only notice that your experience is changing. The things you used to like, are no longer so much fun, the things that used to make you happy before, slowly lose their meaning. You feel dissatisfied, perhaps stressed and alone, misunderstood. In the meantime, your attention is focused on 'wanting to be happy', while your inner landscape is getting darker and darker. Eventually it might be so dark that the world outside doesn't even exist anymore, not anymore in you...

The depressive gestalt makes an inner world that closes you off from the outside world and others. There aren't any landmarks left in that world. In Chapter 11 *Dark Landscape* you could practice with *In the darkness* how it is to be in a completely dark room without exit.[47] Now imagine the following: You are sitting in a totally dark room, no trace of light comes in, you have no idea where an exit is and if there is an exit at all. You are alone, in darkness and you continue to operate with your old (not too clever either) way of thinking.[48] The only thing you appear to want and be able to think of is 'just to be happy' (read:

---

47 Other descriptions also appear: 'floating in space alone', 'feeling down', 'total void', 'stuck' and so on.
48 Please, keep in mind that there are gradations of dark. From light to grey and black.

wanting to be, as a matter of course, in a constant pleasant state of contentment). 'Simply being happy' doesn't exist in that room at all! The world outside that space (the world where being happy may exist) no longer exists. Despite that inner truth, you continue to pursue your old desires. To begin with, happiness couldn't be made concrete and, in addition, turns out to be an impossible wish. Many people quite naturally strive for a life full of happiness and 'wanting to be happy'. This ultimate desire in combination with what you now know about the depressive landscape makes clear how weird that desire really is.

To be able to influence our inner landscape and free ourselves from the hindrances of that landscape, it is important to stand still, get close, in order to better grasp and experience what your inner landscape looks like. This exploration, however tough perhaps, is possibly the greatest gift you can give yourself to meet your real needs. Because if you do not get to know your landscape you will not discover what you are trapped in.

Imprisoned or free

Viktor Frankl, concentration camp survivor and writer of the book *Man's Search for Meaning* was amazed at the fact that, as he called it, there were 'two types of people' in the concentration camp: decent and indecent.[49] There were people who were 'already dead' before they entered the camp and there were people who, as he said, 'stayed alive until the gas chamber door opened'.

> 'When we are no longer able to change a situation, we are challenged to change ourselves.'
>
> Viktor E. Frankl, *Man's Search for Meaning*

Frankl, a very acute observer of human behaviour, was aware that both groups interpreted the same circumstances in a completely different manner. He was very curious as to why that was so. In the camp freedom was obviously an important theme. As time passed, he began to realize that people reacted differently to the same restriction of freedom. Some people concluded that the camp was the end and gave up, where others were more energetic than ever to hold on to what they considered important.

This unique interpretation has to do with the meaning that is ascribed to an experience.[50] This makes meaning a crucial element of how we experience our experiences. Meaning determines whether we go towards or away from somewhere, love or loathe something, regard something as

49 Viktor Frankl, *Man's Search for Meaning: An introduction to Logo therapy*, 1945-1978
50 See Chapter 8 *The five assumptions about depression*.

good or bad.[51] Meaning determines our experiences and in that sense you can say, like Frankl, that: 'The only freedom we really have is the freedom of choice that enables us to decide what something means to us.'

When we are stuck in our states of mind, we get important information about what something means to us. What something means to us can explain why we behave the way we do. At the moment that you are going to investigate what meaning you give to experiences and events, you can wonder whether these meanings work for or against you. Ultimately, that should lead to the realization that you yourself (and no one else) have linked this unique meaning to this particular experience. When you begin to realize that something doesn't have meaning just like that, but that you attribute meaning, you can reclaim that ability. And an owner can decide what something means.

From 'just' meaning to meaningfulness

If a depressed person misses anything, it is... meaning.

Giving meaning is important to all of us (even if you don't think so) and when you feel down you know like no other that experiences lose their colour. The meaning you give to your experiences will ultimately deeply influence whether something is nice and meaningful or not. The more meaningful you can make an experience, the more it will pull you, in a positive and a negative sense. Think of the example of Antonie Kamerling (Chapter 11 *Dark Landscape*) in which he said: 'I always took it very seriously, I thought, I'll never ever come out of this.' Taking it 'very seriously' says something about how much meaning he gives his experience and how tremendously important his sorrowful feelings were for him.

---

51   In neuro-semantics we investigate how you give meaning and how your way of giving meaning influences how you live. For more information about this, see: www.neurosemantics.com.

When we talk about meaning, we are almost automatically talking about meaningfulness, sense of purpose and the meaning of life. Meaningfulness tells us that something is very important to us, that it has much added value, and may even be vitally important. If something is meaningful to you, you have attributed your most important and attractive meanings to that experience. These unique and special meanings create deep feelings. Meaningfulness gives your life meaning and the feeling that you are of added value. The darker your landscape is, the more you get removed from meaning and sense of purpose. The more senseless and meaningless you make your experiences, the darker your landscape becomes.

> 'What confuses man is not facts, but dogmatic opinions about these facts.'
>
> *Epictetus*

Meaningless

As the word says, in meaninglessness the meaning of things has been taken away from them. When things become meaningless, all these beautiful meanings that we (unconsciously) had attributed to the experience have (slowly but surely) disappeared. How do people do that? Because, for example, they have been disappointed. Something that is very important for you and that fails to work out well in the 'real' world can make you disappointed or even cynical. Your values can be violated because something happens in your life by which that what is so important for you is trampled on. Someone can do something to you that causes you not to believe any more in things that were essential to you. Your confidence may be sorely violated. All sorts of things can happen in a lifetime, things that slowly but surely remove the meaning from experiences. Do that long enough and life becomes meaningless. What do you feel then? A void!

Do you get now why 'Cheer up, buddy, we're going to do something fun' isn't going to have much appeal for you when you are feeling down and experiencing emptiness? When you live in a dark world and there is nothing or little outside that world, it is not very realistic to expect that you'll get motivated to do something fun; after all, its meaning has vanished. So, now you might better understand that your loved ones and friends try to motivate you with 'Cheer up, buddy', for, as a matter of fact, they don't live in your landscape. Meaning can only flow again once the door of the dark room comes ajar. As you understand now, meaning also creates feelings and even emotions. You can see emotions as felt meaning.

The meaning of our 'awkward' emotions

In our societies there is a collective taboo on problems. We often give problems the most negative meaning. It's to be expected that this gives us annoying emotions. Problems are, so to speak, denied, ignored and must be resolved as soon as possible. These 'solutions' bring about a shadow side and this shadow slowly becomes more influential.

Because the light (happiness, effectiveness, growth, success) has become so crucial to us, our shadow grows longer and longer. The taboo on failure, mediocrity and the accompanying negative emotions like disappointment, sadness, anger and so on has created an odd reaction to those things that we do not like. What we don't like we try to keep away, suppress, brush away. Precisely because of this attitude, our problem, our pain, sadness and disappointment are greater, more dominant. In the glorification of the light our shadow is born.

This is already evident in our relationship with our awkward emotions as the following example shows well.

PETER

Peter was not comfortable in his skin and felt discontented. He experienced ever more setback in his work as a day trader on the stock exchange and in recent months he kept bothering about it after work. Despite everything he tried, he did not succeed in forcing a little bit of luck to get out of the negative spiral. He felt increasingly frustrated and down.

'What do you come for Peter?'

'I find that hard to say.'

'Oh, can't you put it into words?'

'Yes of course I can, but I don't want to.'

'Ah, then we have a problem.'

Peter starts laughing hard now.

'Yes, if you put it like that. Well, OK, I'm ashamed of this.'

'Of what?'

'Well, I'm sitting with a group of day traders in a room and lately business is a bit down.'

'A bit?'

'OK, quite a bit.'

'Tell me some more about that.'

'Well, I'm losing heaps of money and a few years ago I was one of the better traders at the office. Now I'm haemorrhaging money and I see those guys watching.'

'Oh, those guys look at you?'

'I mean they laugh at me.'

'Is that so?'

'Well, that's the feeling I have. Look, I have lost my confidence a little and do the best I can, but I don't succeed anymore.'

'What is your problem?'

'I'm stuck.'

'Yes, I understand, you are stuck between uncertainty, desire and shame about your inability, is that right?'

'Yes, you can summarize it like that.'

'How are you stuck?'

'What do you mean?'

'Like I'm telling you.'

'Well, as if I'm sandwiched between four walls.'

'Then you're really stuck.'

'Yes, but I'm keeping my back straight, though.'
'Does that help, sandwiched between these walls?'

Due to (in this case) shame the deeper problem is glossed over
and not in the last place for Peter himself. If he is not assisted
in having a critical look at his own experience, he continues
looking for 'solutions' within his own frameworks. Only, his
solutions have little to do with his real problem.

Every meaning Peter assigns to his experience is a
puzzle piece that shapes his landscape. Suppressing his
uncertainty and the shame he feels about his inability
ultimately makes him feel as if 'sandwiched between walls'.
However hard he does his best, he has lost the ability to
escape.

Our issues are hiding; what it is all about is rarely
discussed unceremoniously. This is because the way we
internally assign meaning is not necessarily logical but
more emotional. Each meaning elicits a further meaning
and so it is easy to get stuck when you are ashamed of your
own inability...

Summary
People can persistently pursue vague desires without
realizing that these desires can increase our dissatisfaction.
It is important to stand still, because by becoming more
aware of where you are in your inner experience, it
becomes clearer to you how great the gap is between
your desire and the place where you actually are. Your
inner landscape is determined by, among other things,
the meaning you assign to the experiences you have. The
more negative your meanings, the darker your landscape.
The more meaningless the world outside of you becomes,
the more you feel being cut off. The more cut off, the
less you see the point of it all. The more pointless your
experience becomes, the darker your landscape... In the
next chapter you will explore what symptoms you are
experiencing, so that by observing these symptoms you

are going to get a clearer and more insightful picture of your inner landscape. You need this insight to be able to move in your mental landscape. For, as you know now: the obstacles that you experience in your life are part of your inner landscape, and only when you get to know your inner obstacles, you'll realize what your real goals should be.

14.
Exploring your inner landscape

'Playing hide and seek
is so much fun because
you can be found.'

You may have got a clearer picture of your own inner
landscape by reading this book. Maybe it's not completely
dark but grey, you may experience a closed off room or just
float in space, sit in a pit or stand on a lonely height. Maybe
you only experience a dissatisfaction that you take with
you. There are all kinds of gradations of not being happy:
from the lightest to the darkest.

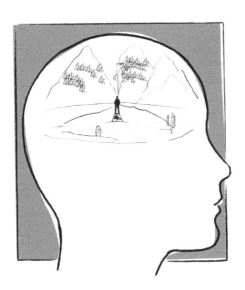

Becoming aware of your landscape is not necessarily fun but *is* necessary. It is necessary because it greatly increases your chances of sustainable change. In this chapter, you're going to explore your landscape as if it were a real landscape.

What is the case?

Just imagine that there is a left, right, front and back when you think of your problem. You are standing on something and there is something above you, just like in 'real' life, but now in the landscape that is your inner representation of the 'real' world. The landscape you see when you close your eyes. Please, discover among all the thoughts that emerge in you, how dark or light your inside world is, how empty or busy it is, whether there are people and how far away they are, whether you shrink from something or something thwarts you, just like in reality. While answering the questions in this chapter, notice what landscape reveals itself to you in your thoughts. After chapter 18 *Good-luck magnet* I take you step by step along through your inner landscape. Is it difficult for you at this time to explore your landscape but do you recognize the gloomy or unhappy mood as characteristic of yourself? That's not a problem, you can do the follow-up exercises anyway. I'll assist you in this process.

Below is a concise version of two questionnaires I've developed.[52] I suggest you take some time to answer these questions and write the answers down on the following pages. The purpose of these questions is to get, for a start, a clearer picture of what you are experiencing right now. From this experience you can become more aware of what you are actually experiencing inside. Your inner landscape can become more visible to yourself. You needn't be uncertain about answering the questions because you do this to discover where your possibilities of moving are. You

---

52 The complete questionnaire is discussed in the training for depression and zest for life coach. Check Wassilizafiris.nl for more information about this.

can start with the *General symptoms list* and, as the word says, this is a general exploration. You can answer these questions globally. Please, take the time for the *Specific symptoms list*. That helps you to get more accurate on your retina what you experience inside. If you discover that you have suicidal thoughts, it is advisable to see your GP or a specialist.

General Gloom Symptoms List[53]

Please, answer the questions below.

→ Describe your everyday states of mind.

→ What do you find difficult and complicated?

→ What are you disappointed about? About who?

---

53 For the complete questionnaire see Depressie en levenslustcoachopleiding, (Depression and zest for life-coach training) Wassilizafiris.nl.

→ How long have you had this?

→ How did this start?

→ How do you sleep? Do you use medication? Do you drink? Do you use drugs?

→ Have you sought help for this before? If so, what exactly did you do? If not, what has stopped you so far to seek help?

Specific Gloom Symptoms List:

Please, answer the questions below and write your answers under the questions to get more insight into how your landscape looks and to what extent you feel dissatisfied, gloomy or even depressed. You may not be able to answer all questions at once. That's not a problem. Read on and come back to this as soon as you have an answer.

Write all the answers point by point:

1. Describe what you are experiencing. What is your problem? What is bothering you?

2. Summarize the whole problem you experience. All in all: What is it you are experiencing?

3. Describe your relationship with the problem you are experiencing. How are you reacting to your problem?

4. When you think of this problem, please describe how you see yourself.

5. When you look in the mirror, what do you see?

6. Tell me something about how you think about people in general?

7. What do you believe about others?

8. What setbacks are you suffering (or have you suffered)? How does adversity affect you?

9. How do you react inside to adversity?

10. When you think of 'tomorrow', or 'will be fun later on...' or 'happiness', 'joy...' what's happening then inside you?

11. If you were to be very specific and tell me what you are experiencing inside when I say 'later on' or 'will be fun later on...' What arises then in you?

12. What do you believe about happiness in your case?

13. And if everything you've said is true, what do you believe about life? What do you believe about the meaning of existence?

When you have written down everything, read all the answers aloud and imagine the following: Suppose, an acquaintance were to have said these things and you see this person in your mind and you would summarize all the things that this acquaintance said. Then look in your mind at this person from a distance: what do you think is the matter with this person?

→ 14 Answer:

Feasibility

Well no, just for a little bit longer then, hoping for a miracle...

It's my experience that it can be very difficult for people to look at their own reality. Wishes, hope and opportunism take it over before you know it.

My client John described that he felt completely on his own, forsaken. He had no real friends and he described that even when he was with acquaintances at a party, he still felt alone.

JOHN
'What do you want to experience instead?', I asked him.
'I would like to have more friends', he said with a big smile on his face that slowly disappeared again.
'Wow, that's a nice goal, hmm, ... for me to get an idea, how feasible is that for you, considering how you know yourself?'
That question unsettled him. After all he had done what was asked of him, and now that was not satisfactory.
'What do you mean', he asked with some irritation in his voice.
'Well, in fact, how feasible is that desire to have more friends?'
'I mean, you know yourself, but from the lonely position you are in, is that desire a feasible exercise for you?'
A few minutes of ostensible silence were followed by a resolute: No. I think that I have wanted this for years and I never ever bring it off.'
'So, once more, what is the tiniest that is or could be feasible for you, which will eventually lead to more friends?'
I heard his head crunch. He was making a tremendous effort to come closer to his real experience: 'I would like to start believing that somewhere there is someone who could like me.'
'Is that feasible for you, bearing in mind how you know yourself?'
'Well, what I could do is focus my attention on signals showing that people could be my friends and people want me around.'
'Is that feasible for you?'
After a short contemplation he said: 'Yes, I can focus on that.'
'Beautiful, that's your goal, no more and no less!'

Feasible

Have a look at your answers from the previous exercise. Ask yourself what you want instead of what's the matter with you. So imagine, you say: 'I want to feel less lonely, so I would like to have more contact with my family.'

Ask yourself a very important question: Have a look at what you want and ask yourself if what you want is feasible for you. Is what you desire feasible for you in your world (the way you are experiencing yourself now and knowing what you do and don't succeed in)?

Write down what you would like to have instead of the problem?
Ask yourself: What, then, is the tiniest thing that is feasible for me?
Write each item down separately and start with no more than four points.

a.

b.

c.

d.

Give yourself pause for thought...

Summary

Now you have reached this point in this book you are all ready to dot the i's and cross the t's. You have, like me, made quite a journey and gained a lot of new ideas, possibly even totally different ideas than you were accustomed to. You have been able to sense how you can face your problems. You have acquired ideas about how your inner landscape can be different from the world outside of you and discovered that you can construct and create meaning. You've learned to see where you are.

Dejection may be one of the most underrastted among the experiences that have a major impact on our lives. A dormant discontent can have a huge effect on our lives. The dark room divulges itself in a poorly lived out life and a dream of a happier life. That desire for a happier life is a desire that gives a lot of hope for a long time, but whatever you do and try out is not leading to that ultimate prize: a happy life. What is going to help you in the daily practice of life is to focus on the tiniest that is feasible for you and take small steps towards it. These smallest steps give you a firm footing for moving around. But for the transformation of your landscape, additional steps are essential. The first thing you need is direction.

Switching off and on

What's on the other side, outside your room? What do you have to focus your arrows on if that is not 'being happy'? You need a star in the sky to be able to navigate so that it is clear what you are looking for when you feel dejected and gloomy. You need a sense of direction like a compass pointing to the north. The realization that you cannot see the north, but you can trust that you are moving in the right direction.

Having a direction helps you to find the crack in your dark room and to set the door ajar a bit more easily. The first ray of light that's needed to be able to move. I know from my own experience that it is important that you can focus on a direction that agrees with the spot where you actually are. The desire for a happy life is not the right direction, hence you still have to deal with disappointment. The surprising part with dejection is that you don't have to set to work at full tilt to find your final direction. Depressive people will not set to work at full tilt anyway, so that's a welcome bonus. To arrive at our final destination, it is necessary to achieve a number of important changes in your inner landscape. As soon as these changes are made, the direction you are looking for will manifest itself. Manifest itself? Yes, manifesting a new direction in life is the result of switching off one thing and switching on another. The depression molecule must be deconstructed to create space for... zest for life and living.

Working on zest for life

How do you set up the conditions for the zest-for-life gestalt to develop? What conditions can we create so that 'the gases can become water' (as described before how water comes into being by bringing together two gases: see Chapter 10, section *Water as gestalt?*)? Do you want to learn how to experience more zest for life and to transform gloom? In the following chapters you will learn step by step how to change your loneliness into a sense of recognition and belonging; how to change a negative self-image into an OK person; and how you finally transform adversity into prosperity. Zest for life is the unique state of mind that can arise when these three needs are fulfilled. Each component adds a unique element and all elements together warrant that light can shine in your landscape.

Accepting
your destiny

15.
Dealing with loneliness

'Life is easier than people think. All you have to do is accept the impossible, do without the indispensable and the suffer the insufferable.'

Kathleen Norris, American poet

Loneliness is one of the triggers of depression and an important part of discontent in people. There are two types of loneliness that have an impact on the emergence of depressive feelings. 1. Loneliness that arises from disturbed family ties: in this form of loneliness, the lack of recognition and welcoming in the family and intimate relationships plays an important role. 2. Loneliness through disrupted relationships in general. In the latter case, convictions created by experiences in the past, like being bullied, play a role. Both forms of loneliness can lead to an even greater sense of loneliness. Existential loneliness: feeling on your own in the world. In this chapter, I'll show you the influence of acknowledgement, acceptance and welcoming on the feeling of loneliness. Moreover, I'll revert to the notion of 'blessed' in Chapter 4 *Being Lucky* because this definition of 'being lucky' is essential in changing feelings of loneliness. You learn how to feel connected, no longer alone. This experience of connection is an essential part of zest for life.

1. Loneliness and Family Ties

Belonging is an essential human need. The urge to belong and not be alone is for some even a reason to kill or die. Think of all those people who join terrorist sects. Being alone and particularly feeling alone is one of the essential components of the depressive gestalt. It is not necessarily the trigger of that gestalt but it certainly is a crucial component. Through my research and having guided people as a coach and trainer for more than twenty-five years, it has become clear to me that our desire for interconnection is an essential lifeblood. Once that lifeline is closed, the road is free for a slowly but surely darker existence. One of the most salient statements a person can make when there is loneliness:

'Even when I'm with friends and loved ones I feel alone.'

When you feel lonely in this way, you experience a cut-off in the connection. As if there is an unbridgeable distance between you and others. Others are felt to be far away or are sometimes completely vanished. A loved one may stand right next to you in the actual world, but far away in your inner landscape. This difference is often observed in awkward or (very) difficult relationships. Frustrations about 'not feeling understood' which can express itself in anger and sadness, and even more isolation and alienation. Some couples may have years of struggle because the connection somehow does not seem to come into being. Often you can find this loneliness back in disturbed family ties, where the ties seemingly can no longer be drawn tighter. Take, for example, family quarrels that often seem to start for no reason at all and whereby people may break off the contact with parents, children or siblings for years. Stubbornly fending off any attempts to patch up the contact can lead to bitterness and loneliness. The loss of friendships or the inability to have long-lasting friendly ties with people can be a consequence of such a shut off connection.

In others this inability to connect shows in an attitude that excludes help. These people steer a course on their own. 'I'll manage on my own, I'll do it all by myself, I just have to do it alone, I'm a self-made man (or woman)...'

This self-made man/woman has developed, what I call, the superman syndrome.[54] The superman syndrome is common. I regularly speak to clients who tell me they 'solve everything themselves' and don't ask for help, even if they have a tough time. Entrepreneurs may also suffer from the superman syndrome. Entrepreneurs often believe that they are right and that others cannot achieve what they can. As a result, they have become successful, but are often very lonely. During the day this isn't very obvious because then 'the light' is on. Then everything is focused on success and for that your best 'I' is required. More results, sales, inspiration and great ties with customers and showing the world how well you are doing. You put the most charming part of yourself in the limelight. You cultivate infallibility, not only for the outside world but also because you have a sacred faith that this is the way to success. After all, the company must ascend to dizzying heights of success. However, in the evening the shadow may come out with sometimes poignant consequences. There is a firm belief that only your most beautiful, most powerful and most independent version can lead to success and happiness. While cultivating this ideal 'I' a shadow has arisen, a side of yourself that you deny, but that undeniably tugs at you. In the recent economic crisis, more entrepreneurs committed suicide than ever, but what is so worrying is that no one noticed how badly these entrepreneurs were doing, in what bad shape they were. They were masterful in exhibiting the light, their grandest and most successful side. In their quest for the ultimate light they had become lonely. In highlighting the light they were unable to talk to anyone about their darkness. Being unable to admit their own fallibility, they had no choice

54 See my Blog *The Superman syndrome* at Wassilizafiris.nl

but to be and remain that successful superman, going on like this until really and truly no one understood them.

An emotional law

Sometimes, people, by changing circumstances such as old age, the death of loved ones, quitting their regular job or no longer being *in the public eye* after a career on stage, may develop loneliness which eventually also leads to the feeling that you are all on your own. If you feel lonely because the family ties are disrupted, you have already had for a while the feeling that you're not understood or that you don't belong. A difficult connection with important people such as father, mother and siblings can make you feel lonely. In an emotional sense, we need to be accepted as we are, but that is definitely not enough. Sound connection arises also through the feeling of being welcomed by your fellow men, and possibly even more relevant: the sense of recognition that you are good as you are. Recognition actually says: 'I see you', 'you're here', 'you're welcome', 'You're supposed to be here'.

'If you are fully acknowledged, you aren't looking for a destination anymore. Then you are at your destination. Being welcome makes life meaningful.'

The message that you are welcome I have also experienced myself as important. My father and mother were never married and when I was nine years old they separated. My father has always stressed that he officially acknowledged me. I never understood why he emphasized that, but it always felt like something good. In Dutch law, acknowledgment of your child is an important legal concept because you are then legally the parent of the child, you and your child become each other's legal heirs, you can also determine your child's surname, your child's gets your nationality... and by the acknowledgment a legal bond is formed between you and your child. 'A family relationship' as it is officially called.[55] You could say that the legal acknowledgment of your child is the legal framework of recognition and welcoming in the psychological sense.

Feeling welcome

In depression it is precisely that recognition that is often not felt and that in my experience is one of the most important seedbeds of the existential loneliness that people can experience.

Some people are firmly convinced that no one likes them, although friends and loved ones are surrounding them. The deep feeling of not being understood by others and even the belief that the world is a bad place, are all symptoms of the profound sense of not feeling acknowledged.

Feeling wanted already begins at conception and pregnancy. In its ultimate form, this feeling is created by the full acknowledgement of you as a complete human being in this life. This full acknowledgement of you as a complete person opens the way to closeness, the sense of belonging, and, what's more, the sense that you are supposed to be here. Eliminating any doubt as to whether you have a place in the family, whether you are associated with some parent or other and life in general. When that deep feeling awakens in someone, the meaning of life is no longer a quest in many cases. Why is that so? Because when you are fully acknowledged, fully received, as you are, just right, then you are not looking for a destination anymore, then you have arrived at your destination. Being wanted and accepted makes a life meaningful.

55 https://www.lawsociety.org.uk/practice-areas/family-children/

Connection and addiction

In the very interesting article by Johan Hari *The likely cause of addiction has been discovered, and it's not what you think*, Hari describes a surprisingly new discovery of the mechanisms of addiction. Experiments with animals and humans show that drugs such as cocaine (one of the most addictive drugs) use a possibly different addiction mechanism than hitherto thought. The average person and specialist will say about, for example, a cocaine addiction that the addictive component is chemical. Until now, it has been assumed that the chemical composition of cocaine is such that our brains cannot resist the stuff, and because it is a chemical process conscious choices play no or little role of significance. However, new research shows something remarkable: Once you get a rat or person out of the addiction context and place them in a context where connecting with others plays a central role then the rats and the people give up the drug within a few days![56] This remarkable discovery places addiction in a completely new light. Conversely, this could mean that addiction suggests an unconscious need for connection and closeness to others, and as soon as that link with others is restored the addiction need disappears!

From being acknowledged to being blessed

One of the descriptions of 'being lucky' from Chapter 4 *Being Lucky* is 'feeling blessed'. We know this term mainly from religious descriptions, baptism ceremonies and such matters. However, truly being welcome in the family seems to have something to do with the same blessing. It is the approval that you are there, the welcome and acknowledgment that you are good as you are, which cause you to experience closeness with the important loved ones around you. The state of mind that opens the way to that sense of blessing is a sense of being fully acknowledged. 'Acknowledgement' implies recognition, approval and

56 Johann Hari, *The Likely Cause of Addiction Has Been Discovered, and It Is Not What You Think*, Huffington Post, 20 januari 2015

adoption. As a father acknowledges his child and, as is stated in various religions that God accepts man, there is a blessing in acceptance, a welcome that not only embraces what is, but demonstrates that you are seen as a human being, recognized and acknowledged in your existence. And it is precisely this blessing and welcoming in life that is a crucial life element! Due to this, the connection with loved ones and the feeling of closeness can be experienced by us. By experiencing yourself that you are blessed with acknowledgement and approval and that you are good, exactly as you are, a foundation is laid for the ability to experience connection and closeness with others.

Acceptance versus acknowledgement

Acceptance or resignation is the ability to embrace a circumstance without emotion. While accepting a given situation, you let go of your expectations and resign yourself to the state of affairs at that time. Acceptance in spirituality, mindfulness and Acceptance & Commitment therapy (ACT) is the willingness to embrace a situation in the realization that it is unalterable. Acceptance may also have an indifferent element in it, 'it doesn't matter', and a transitoriness. The obstacle you accept is of a temporary disposition, a passing thing, which makes it relatively easy to accept. Acknowledgement goes a step further in a psychological sense. Where acceptance 'embraces', 'disregards' and 'ceases combat', acknowledgement does the same and more. Acceptance and acknowledgement both tolerate a situation or experience. Both states of mind resign themselves to a situation and tolerate the experience in a neutral way, 'you resign yourself to it as a fait accompli.' Acknowledgement, on the other hand, expresses a positive appreciation for what you are embracing, unlike 'tolerate', which implies an indirect rejection. And in this rejection is contained an important difference. Acknowledgement includes welcoming the situation you have to accept. Acknowledgement is timeless, an awareness of: 'This is my destiny and this is all I have to get by on.'

Since antiquity it has been incontrovertible that the quest for connection is one of the most important human motives. This need is even so great that we have created a grand role model for it, or this role model has found us (depending on what you believe). When it comes to acknowledging and accepting us as human beings, the greatest role model that many people have is God. In every religion God stands for the ultimate source of love and acceptance. It could even be said that the act of welcoming human beings with open arms in full love and acknowledgement is one of the central elements of belief in a God and the concomitant strain of thought. To understand the grandeur of this, you don't even have to be a believer.

I myself have not been brought up religiously and I think I have a fairly neutral view of religion. This does not alter the fact that I can appreciate the psychological significance of a religious aspect. Especially when it offers a promise of no longer feeling alone. Transmuting the deep sense of loneliness that has been brought about by a disrupted intimate connection, calls for a restored sense of wholehearted acceptance. Acknowledgement heals our capacity to connect and experience closeness. In the process below you can replace the word 'God' with what you believe in. And if a God is too remote from you, you may replace God with someone you find very generous. Someone who is or was an example of loving acceptance to you. Maybe you had a grandmother who gave you the feeling of being fully acknowledged, or you know someone like that. Possibly even another religious example. As long as the sense of acknowledgement attending it is strong.

Acknowledged and blessed

Just imagine what it would be like to look from the grandeur of God or an almighty being like God at humanity, with a great sense of acknowledgement, and this God says as it were: 'I see you', 'you're here', 'you're welcome', 'you're supposed to be here'.

Would you like to feel fully acknowledged and accepted? Do you want to feel connected, feel that you belong here, no longer alone, but seen and acknowledged? If your answer is yes, do the following:

1. Imagine that you can look at the world through the eyes of 'God'. Just pretend this is possible. Just fantasize this for a moment. Notice how you know inside that you can look at the world with that grandeur. Give yourself permission to do so. Realize how grand your view is...

2. Then become aware that as God you look at people with a certain look, namely with the look of total love, of full acknowledgement and blessing. Immerse yourself in the fantasy, just pretend. Overcome your bashfulness. Notice how you know that you are looking at humanity with this look. Notice what you experience when you look at humanity with the look of loving acknowledgement, without judgement. The sense of acceptance and acknowledgement implies that some things may not be fun, but that you welcome them as well, as a sense of destiny.

3. Now think back to the day you were born and keep looking through the eyes of God. Imagine that you can see your birth, but now through the eyes of God. Look through the eyes of full acceptance and acknowledgement at yourself when you were born. Keep watching that newly born baby with that grand, all-encompassing look of loving acknowledgement. And while you're watching this baby you think: 'I see you', 'you're here', 'you're welcome', 'you're supposed to be here'. Acknowledge and welcome that baby who has just been born, with all that is good and less good, acknowledge everything, acknowledge the baby exactly as she or he is, without any judgement. Welcome all aspects of the baby... Do this for a few minutes.

4. Step now, as it were, out of the God image and change perspective. Become the baby, the tiny little baby you were then. Imagine how it feels to be a new-born baby (if necessary, just pretend). Imagine how it feels to be looked at (as a baby) with the eyes of full acknowledgement. Feel how it feels to be fully welcomed, fully acknowledged, just right, connected. Hear in your mind the words: 'I see you', 'you're here', 'you're welcome', 'you're supposed to be here'.

Received

After this experience, take the time to let sink in what this means and how it feels to feel completely received. The sense of recognition, being welcome and even blessing by having been watched through the eyes of acknowledgement, has a wondrous and even 'disruptive' effect on feelings of loneliness. Being watched like this causes you to know that there is someone for you.

Bullying

Depressive people can also have extreme beliefs that are objectively untrue but are felt at a deep level and are decisive for the choices the person makes. At a photo exhibition in London I saw a photograph of an Indian eunuch (a castrated man) with the caption: 'I hate people, I want to die'. This man had not only been castrated by others but had afterwards also been mistreated and bullied a large part of his life because of his sexlessness. Exclusion and rejection are the opposite of acknowledgement and can have a strong impact on how you experience others and the world. It is weird that contemporary synonyms for depression, like for example dejection, downheartedness and gloominess refer to feelings of discouragement, sadness, despondency and dismay. These are all feelings and experiences without any cause, you have it or you don't. This has not always been the case.

In the thirteenth to fifteenth century, the meaning of depression was: to press down, crush, humiliate, and weaken. The even older Latin definitions included, in addition to the medieval descriptions, words like injustice, push on, reject and decrease in value. The striking difference between the old and modern definitions is that modern definitions lay the problem with the person him- or herself (you feel dejected or you are down, you are gloomy) whereas the original definitions describe the true nature of depression, which is what causes the depression. You are being humiliated, weakened, rejected and so on. Something is being done to you. It is my experience that many depressed people indeed experience this literally in this manner. Many of my depressive clients indeed say they have given way under pressure, humiliation and disappointment. The sense that the world or others have brought misery on them. Something that ultimately couldn't be counterbalanced by anything. Viewed like this, depression gives an important clue as to what it is and how it arises. When we realize this, we get more grip on depression.[57]

Bullying is pre-eminently behaviour that can arouse depressive feelings at a later age for various reasons. When you are bullied, you are rejected as a person, which is, as said before, the opposite of acknowledgement. Bullying often takes place in groups with the aim of humiliating, weakening and rejecting the other. Many of my clients talk about the injustice done to them and are often very emotional about it, even though this injustice has taken place a long time ago. Feeling down (in a literal and figurative sense) is also much easier to explain when you feel crushed or humiliated. The feelings of injustice evoked by the humiliations are often 'passive' feelings. By passive I mean that these can be strong feelings in which you can feel completely helpless, for nothing can be done

---

57 The Oxford Dictionary of English Etymology, and several online dictionaries

about the inflicted injustice. It's too strong, too big, or simply cannot be put right any more. Another reason why bullying can be such an important trigger for depression is that you are usually rejected as a person in bullying. You're ugly, or fat, you name it. In any case, the way you are is usually not good. This rejection of a person at identity level we'll see back in Chapter 16 *I'm OK*. Finally, you can say that bullying is something structural, something that takes place over a longer period of time. That is similar to the experience of constant setback as will be discussed in chapter 17 *From setback to prosperity*. In the end, being bullied can lead to difficult relationships with others.

2. Loneliness and disrupted relationships

People with depressive thoughts often have a tough time socially. One remains emotionally remote and connecting is a challenge. The natural reaction of these persons is to flee even more into loneliness. Looked at in this way, a dark room is an excellent place to hide, just a pity that you can no longer find the exit yourself...

Through all kinds of experiences, we can develop beliefs about others and how others see us (see more about this in Chapter 16 *I'm OK*). These beliefs determine how we are in relation to others or not, our proximity or distance and the degree of intimacy that we can have.

Entrepreneurship at lonely heights

There are many stories of entrepreneurs who have gone bankrupt several times to eventually become successful anyway. Successful Hollywood films often follow the same scenario: the hero falls from his pedestal, scrambles to his feet and topples once more from his pedestal, comes to a dead end, changes his life round and finds a new path and a new love. The hero turns out to be human, fragile and wanting to be together with others. Going bankrupt is often seen as a strength in the United States. Fall, rise to your feet and carry on again.

A special form of loneliness that can lead to depression is loneliness due to status. Status (read: being looked up to) is very important to some people. Money, a wonderful job, expensive home, a good education and nice appearance, all these things can give some status or other to the person. It makes you special, exceptional and important, but 'special' people turn out to be the loneliest people in the world. Why? Because of their supremacy, contact with 'the ordinary people' is out of the question, and that difference in stature can be very lonely. The need for appreciation is greater than the connection with people, but that is paradoxical, because the need for appreciation is precisely in the hope that a connection will then arise as a result...

The contradiction that takes place in the mind of the person is the following: There is a very great need for connection and being together, at the same time the person has the conviction that by being special you are revered by others. You will be appreciated if you excel, are better than the other, or richer, prettier and smarter. There is a deep desire for connection and closeness. 'Having everybody at your feet' is the closeness that is at your disposal. The tricky thing is that this kind of closeness is conditional, you always have to do something for it. This translates into ever more training, amassing riches, outward show or simply trespassing beyond your own boundaries to be appreciated by others. The status that creates the constant improvement will make you stand on an ever-higher footing, with the distance between you and others nothing but increasing. Your desire for connection is steadily becoming more difficult to achieve and the only method to connect that you are experiencing is gaining even more status. As has already been said, if your status is important for you, you are often lonely.

Off your pedestal

The status-sensitive person stands in a mental-emotional sense on a pedestal, a platform above others. And what is the unconscious endeavour? That the person is looked up to, because if people look up to you there is appreciation, and if there is appreciation, you belong, you are special, special enough to be embraced by the other and the group. The problem with this approach of connection is that the person in question is already lonely by definition, if only because, in a mental sense, he or she is on a raised platform: the special place this person wishes to hold. The distance between the person and others cannot be bridged because the more prestige, the more distance. You often see this problem with celebrities: being at the centre of interest and needing attention from the public to feel good, while at the same time feeling tremendously alone. Successful entrepreneurs can also experience this: Tremendously keen to set up a magnificent company, but when they finally have everything they ever coveted, it is beginning to dawn on them that they have no connection with other people. All the glory is suddenly empty, without intrinsic value.

Status-sensitive people often talk in private about the fear of being exposed, making a poor show, as if they already realize that they can fall from their self-created pedestal if they aren't careful. As a result, they have to work harder and harder to stay on the pedestal. For tumbling off the pedestal is 'the worst thing there is'. This not only indicates failure, but also lays bare what it is all about, namely the loneliness that drives everything.

In this manner, setbacks or bankruptcies may be a blessing. If the person, just like the Hollywood hero, learns to show his or her vulnerability and realizes that connection isn't created by high esteem, but by vulnerability, then a setback which causes you to fall off your pedestal may be the greatest gift you can receive. For in this way, your beliefs about what creates connection and how others experience you, can be adjusted again. Finally 'among people'.[58]

58 See my blog *Ondernemen op eenzame hoogte* (*Doing business on lonely heights*) at Wassilizafiris.nl

Beliefs and convictions

Beliefs are interesting structures and we know that beliefs, by definition, do not necessarily fit in with reality. We can be firmly convinced of something without it being consistent with reality. For example, if you are convinced that no one is to be trusted, you are probably on your guard in contact. But the belief that no one is to be trusted is not objectively true because most of us know someone who is trustworthy. Therefore, beliefs – convictions – don't necessarily correspond with reality. However, they are real for the person who has the conviction. We can hear beliefs by listening to how you formulate your experience. Examples of beliefs are: 'I don't belong', 'I'm outside', 'I'm alone in the world', 'You don't understand me'.

All these ideas lead us to experience some form of loneliness. The disadvantage of a belief is that we continue to look for evidence that the belief is true, though usually this happens unconsciously. The following example shows that convictions can have us completely unconsciously in their grip.

> *HANS*
>
> *Some years ago, I received Hans in my office. He was sent to me by his employer. Hans would rather not talk to anyone, but his boss had said that it was sink or swim for him, so he was somewhat motivated. He told me he was a manager at a company and had had a rage attack towards a colleague. His colleague had been so frightened that everyone thought it wise to call in help.*
>
> *'It didn't amount to anything much', he said. 'Getting angry, for once, should be possible, shouldn't it. One can also be touchy, can't one?'*
> *Amused, Hans told me that he would like to learn some techniques to communicate more subtly with others so that he would have problems of this kind less quickly in the future. I tried several times by asking deeper, but I came up against a subtle but steadfast wall. This made me suspect that there was*

more going on than he told me initially. It seemed sensible to go into the stuff he had a great deal of confidence in: the best tricks. I offered him my best tricks to start practicing with and he was very content with that. A few weeks later he came back.

'Well that hasn't helped at all, worse still, I applied the tricks, but they did not do what I wanted and I got into a quarrel again.'

He seemed somewhat more desperate this time so I grabbed my chance to dig deeper.

'Have you ever experienced this before? I mean such a big quarrel at your work, or is this absolutely the first time?'

'No', he said immediately, 'at my previous job I was thrown out. That's why I thought now: Let me do something about it.'

'And was that the only other experience?'

I continued to ask these kinds of questions and a world unfolded of events riddled with quarrels, anger and disrupted relationships. Initially in the realm of work, going back to his first job, and then also in the private sphere, at school and at home. After thirty minutes of telling stories about one after another example of quarrelling I asked Hans: 'Seeing that again and again you've had all these experiences with people, what conclusion have you drawn from your relationship with other people?'

'People are bad, they are not to be trusted!' he said resolutely.

He was shocked by his 'pronouncement', but realized that what he had just stated was completely true for him. He has always had this conviction in his system without being aware of it in this way.

'People are bad, they are not to be trusted', I retorted.

'Now I understand that you can be so angry with others. You always find evidence that you can never have a relationship of trust, that you must always be on your guard.'

'Yes', he said. 'That's true, I'm always ready to go into an attack. I'm actually always kind of defensive, expecting something nasty.'

After some meandering and scrutinizing what all this meant for him, his relationships and his life, we started looking for a new conviction, one that might help him to enter into better and more satisfying relationships. Since he couldn't think of anything,

I made a suggestion: 'What if you were to believe that others are in principle to be trusted?'
This proposition appealed to him, because then he could still proceed with caution, but was open to establishing contact. After some work with the old and the new conviction[59] he walked out the door with another look in his eyes. 'What if people are in principle to be trusted', he muttered while walking out of my office.

That evening my phone rang. It sounded very busy and noisy and I could hardly hear who it was until I recognized Hans's voice. 'I have to tell you something, I'm walking in the middle of the station square, in the middle.' Hans paused as if he was expecting applause and said one more time: 'I'm walking in the middle.' 'What do you mean?', I asked him. 'For years I have been walking along the side of the building at the square, alongside the building, do you understand? I'm walking today for the first time in the middle. I never realized that this went so far, thank you!' Before I could say anything the line went dead.

What we believe about others can make us particularly lonely. By summing up experiences we draw conclusions and unconsciously they form our beliefs. Because a belief by definition is not a truth, but a conclusion, a generalization, beliefs can be extraordinarily restrictive, and certainly beliefs that slowly but surely make you lonely.

It is lonely in a dark room

It is quite extraordinary to realize that the end result of all the elements of the depressive gestalt is a 'dark chamber'. In this dark room you are obviously alone, you do not even know where the exit is and, as said, this is quite a good hiding place. You have withdrawn owing to an external suffering or to what others have done to you. You don't have any influence on the light in the room.

---

59 Please note that changing beliefs can best be done with the help of an expert.

That is beyond your ability, even outside your room. You have to go through a kind of suffering hoping that the light will be put on for you. This extreme dependence on something or someone outside yourself causes you to become more and more lonely. People who are hoping for an external miracle are often also prone to New Age-like ideas in which 'unexplained' phenomena and forces can have great influence on the person. From hand reading, to photo readings, energies and auras to subgroups and drugs and other (high) sensitivities. Now I don't want to say that there aren't more things in heaven and earth than we can perceive, however the unhappy persons in dark rooms believe in external forces for the wrong reasons. The humiliators have proved themselves right, you have no influence. This way you become slowly but surely lonelier, even less understood and alone. The solution? Influence! Find the light in your own room, don't wait until it happens, put the light on, warm your heart (more about this in *I'm OK*) and take initiative, follow your own path.

Lonely and connected

Connection is an essential part of our being human. In our book *IK BEN niet alleen op de wereld* (*Meaningful profit* is the English version) Ben Steenstra and I have described the stages of connection that people need to be fully alive: connection with yourself, connection with others, connection with something larger than ourselves. Connection is the lifeblood for us and connection with others even more so. One of the most powerful things we have at our disposal to make a connection is vulnerability. Vulnerability is the ability to tell others what you actually would rather not want them to know. It is the ability to admit that you have made mistakes, have hurt people. Vulnerability is actually about the need behind your behaviour, about being able to express once more the need behind your behaviour. Marshall Rosenberg clarifies in *Non-violent Communication* how you learn to express and communicate your need once more. That is essential, because to learn to express your real need, for example to a loved one, makes it possible that your beloved can connect (again) with you. Being vulnerable and expressing your real needs means that you don't have to justify yourself, you don't have to explain why you did something wrong or something stupid. You can also stop blaming. Vulnerability and expressing your real needs you can learn and practice. Here are some tips you can start with today.

Tips

❶ To strengthen your sense of connection, vulnerability is essential. Look, you needn't cry at every conversation, but saying what you are really experiencing, showing your authenticity, is a vulnerable act. Vulnerability is excuseless, expressing your real need. Go and practice this. Tell others that you don't understand things rather than pretending you do. Say that you are really bothered about something rather than acting tough and don't invent reasons why you act the way you act. Being vulnerable is already more than enough reason for connection.

❷ Use words that create trust such as: I was wrong, you're right, I shouldn't have done that, I'm sorry.

❸ Watch the videos of Marshall Rosenberg on YouTube about communication between partners. There you can find handles that help you connect more deeply with your partner.

Summary

Feeling connected is an essential component of zest for life. Our sense of connection can be disrupted by issues in bonding with our families in which the sense of acknowledgement and being understood is lacking. The sense of connection, and thus feelings of closeness, can be restored. The experience of acknowledgement and blessing can wake you up again so that you can feel connected again, no longer alone and even supported. Depression may not only be a phenomenon of the person itself, but a state of mind that can be partly triggered by external forces such as humiliation and oppression. The sense of having no influence that arises from this creates 'passive' feelings. Strong feelings nothing or little can be done with. The forces needed for that are simply perceived as too great. This explains why depressive people can sit in a pit (lower than others) in their inner landscape or trapped in a space without exit (others have the power). Reopening yourself to vulnerability is something that is in your power. Allowing yourself to be vulnerable is one of the means that you do have to restore the connection to others. Vulnerability gives you influence again.

Zest for life and connection go hand in hand. In the next chapter you will explore how your self-image affects the depressive landscape and how by updating your self-image you can increase your zest for life.

Embracing yourself

16.
I am OK

Unhappy: A feeling of dissatisfaction that often goes with depression, strain, anger or sadness.[60]

Our self-image can change and so it does. Usually this change is a slow transition to a 'new I'. Having children, for instance, changes our self-image of 'free man' (or woman) into father or mother. That is a steady process. You already knew what you were, but you become more than you were. The speed at which our identity adapts to changing circumstances varies from person to person and also depends on the circumstances. In the example of children, I often have conversations with clients in which the mother has already updated her self-image to 'mother' at a much earlier stage than the father. New fathers often put that off for a few years with all the associated possible conflicts in the relationship. Your self-image in depression is very relevant, but it is not just your self-image that may be a trigger for depression. It's a suddenly changing self-image that can trigger depression. In depression, the self-image has changed overnight. And by 'overnight' I mean that suddenly you experience a difference between who you have become and who you thought you were... This creates a fight in yourself. In this chapter I take you along to a picture of how we form our self-image and I'll go into examples of an abruptly altered self-image. I'll discuss how rejection and 'not belonging' can contribute to a negative development of your self-image. 'Sectarianism' is an example in which the self-image of a person mainly develops according to the wishes of the sect leader. Living

60 http://www.encyclo.nl/begrip/ongeluk (concept/misfortune)

in conflict with yourself and in dissatisfaction with your life can lead to depressive feelings. Ultimately, your self-image is formed by how you think about yourself, but also by how others think about you. Your self-esteem is determined by these factors. Self-esteem is an important endeavour because it will eventually help you to erase the discord in yourself and the effects of the rejection by others. This chapter takes you along on the road to self-acceptance, more self-esteem and an updated self.

> 'Some actors couldn't figure out how to withstand the constant rejection. They couldn't see the light at the end of the tunnel.'
>
> *Harrison Ford*

This isn't me

We all have an identity, a sense of who we are, a self-image. Our identity is a pivot from which we discover and shape our lives. The formation of our identity begins with our name, our gender, our origins, family structure and so on. In order to function in a healthy way, we need a constant self-image, one that we do not live in odds with. 'Not living in odds with' is a crucial part of a person's healthy functioning. For, as soon as we reject parts of our self-image, disapprove of it or even hate it, problems arise and one of those problems is dejection.

ROBERT

Robert is following a training of mine and during the module about identity 'Who am I?' he says he's feeling down, without zest for life. He does not understand, because he has everything. An attractive wife he is fond of, a successful job with an income that meets his wishes, everyone is healthy and yet... We get to talk and he tells us that things are getting more and more difficult. He is self-employed but is increasingly averse to visiting customers or networking. Time and again he feels dissatisfied, restless, lets things slide.

'Unlike me', he says.

'Since when has this been going on?'

'Well, about eight months, maybe nine.' He looks at me quizzically.

'What happened just before you started feeling like this?'

After a long silence he gives me a probing look. 'The morning of my 50th birthday', he says with tears in his eyes.

'My six-year-old son entered the bedroom with the birthday cake, he embraced me and over his shoulder I looked at myself in the mirror of the bedroom. Then it started.' Suddenly he saw himself in his reflection in the mirror in a way he hadn't seen before. 'THIS ISN'T ME', he yells at me.

He tells me that he had always felt youthful and had lived it. The moment he embraced his six-year-old son on his 50th birthday caused a sudden, dramatic shift in how he experienced himself. He saw his grey hair and realized at that moment that he might not see his son grow very old. The combination of his outward appearance, 50th birthday and the finiteness of how he would live to see his son's life, and of how his son would see his, made him in one go aware of the fact that he was old. Much older than he had previously thought possible. 'This isn't me', he stammers again. This moment of shock and confusion requires an acute adaptation of Roberts self-image. An adaptation that Robert cannot yet make. For in that case he would be compelled to give up too much of himself in order to have what he sees tally with how he experiences himself. The acute shift of his self-image is too great and so he gets stuck in denial.

'We need a constant self-image, one that we don't live at odds with.'

The creation of our self-image

All in all, our self-image is a concept, an idea. No one has ever found an identity or self-image in the street, so we could conclude that 'identity' and' self-image' are concepts, ideas in our minds. More specifically, we can say that our identity is moulded by the meanings we attribute to who we think we are. 'I'm stupid', for example, is a generalization about your ability to think, reason and analyse, which is tagged as 'stupid'. Once that meaning has become a fact, you're probably going to avoid complicated tasks, or you might choose to do Pre-vocational Secondary School instead of Higher General Secondary Education etc. The meaning you attach to who you are is nourished by meanings that you assign yourself to who you are, but also the meanings that your environment (parents, family, friends) assign to you. A teenager is hanging about in the kitchen, mother can no longer put up with it: 'You're driving me crazy with that bustle, you're such a restless child.' What is first, the child's agitation or is the child restless because her environment has defined her so?

Puberty is one of the moments that our self-image is moulded. While you are feeling out where you do or don't belong, part of your identity is generated. Unfortunately, adolescents are often busy deciding which people are dumb or looking bad, and which ones they don't want to be connected with. In the constant description of 'Who and what is *not*', the adolescent does not get a sense of 'who or what *is*'. Then you mainly get clues about who you are *not*, but not about who you *are*. This leads to the need to belong to special groups, which don't appear to be quite the thing either. As a result, some young people land up in 'tough' but incipient criminal groups, or come into contact with drugs, simply because that 'cool' group is doing that. While it often turns out that the adolescent is not at all happy with what that group does: 'For it's just not me'.[61] Identifying yourself in this way is difficult because

---

61 Steve Andreas, *Transforming Your Self: Becoming Who You Want to Be*, 2002

developing your own self-image is easier if you know what you want than if you are focused on what you don't want.

Not belonging

As I noted in the previous chapter, our primary- and secondary-school years are important for us. These are the years when you are developing a steadily brighter picture in mind of who you are. In those same years at school it is important for a child to belong and to be accepted for who you are. During these fragile years, a number of elements in the development of your self-image play a major role:

→ Rejection

→ Acceptance

→ Appreciation

→ Admiration

In a group you can simply be rejected: you do not belong, you are not OK as you are. As has been said before: bullying is an excellent example of rejection. The bullying group rejects you and makes it clear that you do not belong. You are obviously not good enough. You are conspicuous by how you don't belong.

There are also fellow pupils in the classroom who don't stand out and are left alone, the kind of colourless people who are simply accepted in the group. Not special, not annoying, they are just there. Then you have pupils who are special, the pupils who are valued for some quality. Those are the children who are first chosen for gym because they are so skilful with the ball. You know the type. In the end you have special pupils who are good at everything, attract attention in one way or another, special children, children who are secretly admired.

These four facets of how children judge each other (rejection, acceptance, appreciation, admiration) can later play a role in the children's inner world.

Outside, inside

You can reject facets of yourself by constantly judging a part of yourself as bad, not cool, ugly and so on. In this way, a discord develops between you and your self-image, which is difficult to break through. Why? The rejection suggests that a part of who you are is not good enough. Moreover, we have learned we should change what is not good about ourselves instead of accepting it. This process of change can take on remarkable proportions. Outward appearances, for example, that are not good enough should be different, ears that stick out should be flush with the head, pouches under the eyes flat again, noses like a doll. Unfortunately, it happens all too often that when an appearance has been cosmetically improved then some time later it will be another part of the body's turn and another... What started out as a happy correction ends in a rebuilding. The final result? Dissatisfaction. Dissatisfaction because correcting the outside is different from correcting the inside.

As in chapter 2 *Emotions and a happy life* has been described, perfectionism is an enemy of happiness. But perfectionism is in many cases not just a quest for 'better'. The more you think like a perfectionist, the greater the chances of inner struggle. And it is the battle with who we are that is ultimately so exhaustive. Research shows that perfectionism is a stronger indication of suicide than gloom. Why? A perfectionist can only do one thing in the end, fail! The relentless battle you are fighting with yourself by keeping your dark sides in the darkness in the hope that you can become something that you are not, eventually creates an unbearable field of tension. Continual failure, discouragement and disappointment, which may in many cases ultimately lead to one thing: crisis.[62]

Perfectionism is in many cases accompanied by an inability to deal with criticism and can therefore be a signal of a negative self-image that is denied. 'You should not take it so personally', the man says to his wife after he has told her that she is slightly fatter than some time ago. That remark proves to be the beginning of a fierce debate culminating in a quarrel and ultimately a very sad woman on the couch. 'Why do you always make this kind of thing so personal?' says the man. 'I can't say anything to you without you getting all defensive.'

Some people take criticism well, they master the art of hearing criticism as feedback. They keep criticism as a number of facts outside themselves. Outside themselves as a person. May even be curious about it. In others, criticism hits home. Each word is one too many. Often this is because the criticism enters a spot that the person tries to hide, from his- or herself. In that case, the criticism brings to light what you try to keep in the dark, and because another points it out it is extra true. The other has also observed it...

'Sometimes I feel my whole life has been one big rejection.'
Marilyn Monroe

62 Elizabeth Lombardo, *Better Than Perfect: 7 Strategies to Crush Your Inner Critic and Create a Life You Love*, 2014

Dangers to our self-image

There are two dangers to the formation of our self-image:

1. The danger of not belonging, being rejected: Obviously you are not good enough as a person. If only you were different you might belong.
2. The danger of falling short of the standard in your own eyes: thinking in shortcomings about who you are. You're not smart, beautiful, sporty enough.

In each case, you must be different, you must be something you are not now, because what you are now is not good. What is not good must be in the darkness and what we want to be we need to sculpt, shape and create. That must stand large in the light.

'Depression is the ultimate submission.'

Depressed persons feel helpless and hopeless. In the previous chapter it was clearly stated that others may be involved in the onset of depression. Pressed down, humiliated, rejected, it is all injustice that's being done to us. The balance of power is clear: the 'outer' forces are stronger than the inner forces can withstand. There is a fight going on in which submission is central. And depression is the ultimate submission.

In cults and sects you see this phenomenon magnified. The sect leader demands and forces (using the group) the individual to surrender his or her own identity. When these individuals revolt, they are threatened with exclusion, guilt and obligation.[63] As I described previously in *Dealing with loneliness*, my gloomy clients have

63 Frances Peters, Arjan van Dijk, *How do you get the sect out of the former sect member*? From: Special 'Day of the Coach' of the Magazine for coaching, June 2015

surprisingly often experienced that there are, or were at some point in their lives, external forces, making them feel they have no influence. Coercive personalities, such as cult leaders, are not only seen in sects. Coercive behaviour and subjugation is also found in schools (bullying is one example of this), parents, employers and lovers. You can even make yourself so familiar with this coercion that you compulsorily want to change sides of yourself. If you look at a part of yourself with rejection, you have a problem, whichever way you look at it.

Being whole

Your dissatisfaction with yourself, your circumstances and your life make you unhappy. Letting yourself become whole and developing a healthy feeling for who you are requires something very paradoxical: It requires the ability to bring into the light what you want to hide. Becoming whole requires you to stop fighting that which you have long known should be accepted, but instead accept it. Becoming whole requires a completely different attitude than pulling yourself down, blaming, accusing, judging or sabotaging yourself. Becoming whole is actually counter-intuitive. Because what you should do, goes against what you want to do.

Depression is often accompanied by a suddenly changing self-image. Due to some circumstance you become suddenly aware that you are different than you thought you were. Your shadow suddenly comes into the light. Take the example of the man who on his 50th birthday suddenly sees that he is not a young man anymore. Or the example of a top athlete who looks at his knee about which the doctor has said that he can never play football again, 'THIS ISN'T ME', he shouts as he points at his knee. And even the man who in an explosive quarrel gives his wife a slap and says: 'THIS ISN'T ME'. That 'This isn't me' experience not only causes shock but also leads to rejection. That which you are not (yet apparently have turned out to be) suddenly enters your consciousness and you are not happy with what is presented to you.

Tip

Become curious about who you compare yourself with. Do you see, for example, slender people in the street and do you think then: 'They are and I am not?' Do you have feelings of jealousy towards others? Don't you dare to look in the mirror, afraid of what you will see? Do you notice that you hold your tongue even though you have good ideas? Get curious about your way of comparing with others. The more you are occupied with what you are not, but would like to be, the greater the chance that you will reject parts of yourself.

Identity update

The shock you get when you discover who you have become calls for a radical adjustment, an update of who you are. The shift in how you experience yourself has also transformed your fate, your destiny. As already discussed, our self-image is not a constant. We change, who you are changes. It is a given. Your self-image generally changes slowly. This can be a process of years. This not only means that you look at yourself with a different look when you look in the mirror. As soon as you become a father or mother you will notice this too. For a long time, you may try to persevere with your old life or revert to it. Slowly but surely you start to realize that, with a little one, you can't go back to your old life. Caring for your child is forcing you to give in to a new reality and a renewed self-image. A reality where you think in a different manner than before about your responsibilities, life choices, future expectations. And all these adjustments, in turn, require other adjustments. That is quite a chore. A sudden major change in your self-image is, from a mental and emotional point of view, too much of a good thing. Even if you were to have the means to put your perceived identity on an equal footing with your factual identity, most people would still experience resistance to do so. Why? Because that is experienced as too large an adjustment which has to take place in one go. It's not only the person you thought you were who changes then right away, but, what's more, you have to let go of the idea that you still might be able do something about it. Your expectations and plans for the future and the important life choices you'll have to make will all be perceived as simply one size too big. You try to postpone accepting who you have become by means of your dejection. In that way you create a vacuum wherein time seems to stand still.

Time is ruthless in that sense, and if your actual self-image does not change spontaneously, then the awareness thrusts itself upon you that there is only one thing left to do: to embrace who you have become, to embrace what your new destiny is.

However, we can speed up updating our identity and sometimes it is very relevant. Some years ago I was approached via LinkedIn to visit Al Gore in San Francisco. This happened after I had enrolled for a leadership meeting months before. I had never received an answer, so I had forgotten about it. I thought the LinkedIn message was a hoax and had chucked the invitation away. A few weeks later the same invitation was mailed to me again. I was tempted to press the link for the simple reason that I am committed to nature and the environment and I did not want an invitation from Al Gore to pass me by, but even so I removed the mail because a virus on my computer I really didn't fancy. Some weeks later I got the same mail, but now with the message not to delete it and after some doubt I pressed the link. The link appeared to be correct and I was invited to come to San Francisco to participate in a meeting with Al Gore. I seized this opportunity with both hands. Moreover, I had already planned to go to California to finish my training 'Entrepreneur facilitator and master trainer' at the University of Santa Cruz. When I arrived at the university the class was already in full swing and the teacher (and also my mentor) Robert Dilts saw me arrive. I wanted to take my seat quietly, but Robert announced me through the speakers as 'the alumnus who has been invited by Vice President Al Gore'. An applause filled the room and somewhat surprised I walked towards Robert. Robert asked me to come to the stage to explain how I had succeeded in meeting such a celebrity. As I approached him, he made an aside remark. 'Wassili, have you already updated your identity?' That remark, however casually made, was a very relevant remark, as this would usher in a new phase of my life...

To enter a new phase of your life you need an identity update. Instead of continuing to fight with a part of yourself, it is imperative that you become whole again, and becoming whole again is essential to shine light in your darkness.

> 'Even when you are on the right track, you'll get run over if you just sit there.'
>
> *Will Rogers*

The next process, identity update, is divided into three steps to gain insight into how you experience yourself and who you have become. How you experience yourself depends not only on how you perceive and experience yourself, but definitely depends as well on how others see you: Your self-image is a combination of all these perspectives. Updating your self-image is important because it awakens a healthy sense of self-esteem in you and restores the connection with yourself. As a result, you will realize that whatever forces there might be that want to pull you down, suppress or reject you, they have no power to control you if you experience that you are good, good just as you are.

Identity update

Step 1: Looking in the mirror
Stand in front of a mirror and take a good look at yourself (in a literal or figurative sense).

→ When you look in the mirror, what do you see? Are you happy with what you see or don't you recognize yourself? Is the idea that you have of yourself different from what you perceive in the mirror? Have you become aware of a sudden self-realization in the past period? A self-image you are not happy with?

→ Write the answers here:

→ When you look in the mirror, become aware of what you see which you are not happy with.

Answer the following question:
'I see X and I'm not that.'
Such as: 'I see that I have a pot belly and that's not right, I'm not that, I'm a sportsman.'

→ Write down all the differences between how you experience yourself and what you see.

Step 2: Dissatisfaction

Make a list of things you are dissatisfied with. Start with three things about yourself that you are dissatisfied with. Be honest. What do you find stupid of yourself, what do you hate about yourself, do you find ugly? What are you fighting against in yourself?

→ For now, write down three things that you actually have known for a long time you should accept but don't.

1.

2.

3.

Step 3: Connecting with yourself

Now think of the following: Have you ever comforted someone? One of the remarkable things about comforting is that as a comforter you cannot take away the original source of the injury, but that you can be there with your comfort for the emotional pain the person is experiencing. Seen like this comfort is a healing quality. Not so much for the physical wound, but for the emotional wound.

→ Remember one time you comforted someone who was in pain or in sorrow. Get that memory back and notice how you feel when you are comforting. Notice where your attention is, experience how it is to comfort.

→ How can you tell that you are comforting? How do you know inside that you are comforting? What else lets you know? Become aware of how you experience comforting as a state of mind. Notice how comforting feels.

a. Write down the experience:

What do you say to yourself or the other when you are comforting?

→ What do you say to yourself? What do you say in yourself when you feel consolation? Do you say things like: 'It's all right.' 'I'm there for you.' 'No worries, you'll be fine.'?

b. Write down what you say to yourself – your comfort words:

What do you do with your body?

→ What do you do with your body when you feel consolation? Usually when people are consoling, they make an embracing movement or place a hand on a shoulder. Notice what you are doing when you keep thinking of your example of being in a comforting state.

c. Write down what you are doing with your body when you are comforting:

Make sure you have a clear feeling of being consoling. Make sure that this state of mind has at least an 8 in strength on a scale of 0 to 10.

As you continue to feel you are comforting, go back to step 1: *Look In the mirror* and step 2: *Dissatisfaction*.

→ Feel the consoling feeling and focus it on your own feelings of dissatisfaction. Comfort all those feelings and aspects of yourself that you are so dissatisfied with, just as you would another. Embrace them and speak your comforting words from the previous exercise.

→ Comfort all those sides of yourself that you are not happy with *when you look in the mirror* and have dissatisfied feelings about yourself.

→ Probably you meet with resistance in the beginning but keep consoling and think 'I am here for you', 'No worries, you'll be fine'. Keep doing this, repeat your own comforting words, embrace and feel what happens when you comfort yourself.

→ Notice what happens.

How is your inner landscape changing due to this?

→ Take the time to experience this feeling of consolation while all those sides that you prefer to keep in the shadows are consoled. Notice how this changes your inner landscape. Take the time to experience how your inner landscape changes when you fully comfort who you are.

In embrace, you can completely change the relationship with a nasty emotion, by comforting you can change a difficult relationship into a supportive; in this manner you open the way to a better relationship with your own difficult feelings and awkward sides of yourself. In an embrace your problem is going to be yours! In a consoling embrace you do not expect anything, you are just present, for the feelings...

Shame

Self-acceptance opens the door to self-esteem. Self-esteem is the felt realization that you are worthwhile, even if you are not perfect. Therefore, self-esteem cannot be created by how others respond to you because it is your own judgement about yourself. Judging yourself negatively reduces your self-esteem.

How others think about us is of course important to us. Therefore, the feeling of being seen by appreciative eyes also affects our self-awareness. Being a good person, valued and loved, not only influences our experience of belonging, but also the feeling that we matter, that we are of added value in the eyes of others. We need to be seen as human beings, good and meaningful. Unfortunately, we can't always control how others see us. Moreover, our behaviour may have caused us to leave a negative impression on others. How we are perceived is not so much a function of how we are actually perceived, as a function of how we believe we are perceived. In depression, how we are seen by others is relevant because a world that presses you down, suppresses and rejects you, by definition implies that others think badly about you; and the longer that goes on, the more likely it is that you yourself, too, will come to believe that you are bad.

I have already said that our identity is the whole of perspectives about ourselves. Perspectives of yourself about yourself, and how others think and speak about you and how you think others think and speak about you. It is very important to some people how others think and speak about them. The more important that is, the more likely it is you are chiefly busy preventing others from rejecting you. Shame and being ashamed of who you are is one of the foremost emotions which ensures that you cannot embrace yourself as you are. Getting rid of shame is sorely needed to be able to update your own identity.

Transforming shame

Ask yourself:

→ How do others see me?

Gather your ideas of how different people see you. Write down one by one how you experience and think people see you.

1.

2.

3.

4.

5.

Look at all the statements and take all the ideas you've written down together as it were. If all that is written there is true, what kind of film is playing in your mind about yourself?

Describe the film:

→ Look at the statements and the film about yourself through the eyes of others and ask yourself: If all this is true, what kind of person am I in the eyes of others?

Write down:

Ask yourself:

→ What would you like to believe about yourself instead of what you think others now believe about you?

Write down:

Ask yourself:

→ How could I make that belief a reality in my life?

Write down:

→ What are the smallest things you could do daily that would be expressions of the new belief?

Write down:

What could you take heed of so that your new conviction becomes stronger?

Write down:

Being OK

Notice what you are experiencing now that you can experience yourself differently. To feel that you are good, an OK person, it is especially important that you fully embrace yourself again. Rejecting parts of yourself is actually doing just as what the forces outside of you did or do. Break that circle by making yourself whole so you can wholeheartedly say: I am OK.

Summary

Our self-image changes slowly. A too sudden changing self-image can cause an unbridgeable break in our self-perception and thus damage the connection with ourselves. Our self-image is also determined by how others think about us. Belonging and being associated with others is one of our basic needs. If you believe that you are also valuable in the eyes of others, then the world is a lot more attractive. As soon as we face rejection of ourselves or parts of ourselves, our self-esteem starts to sink. After all, self-esteem is the ability to appreciate yourself for who you are. Rejection by others can create in you the conviction that you are not OK, not good enough as you are. These forces outside you can 'subdue' you and awaken a sense of shame in you. Shame inhibits your ability to restore the connection with yourself. For zest for life it is important that you do not live at odds with yourself and that you are connected with yourself in a healthy way. Updating your identity will not only help you to accept yourself as you are, but as a consequence you will also embrace your changed future expectation and your corresponding destiny. These elements help you to experience little by little more zest for life.

In the next chapter you will get acquainted with the influence of setbacks on the depressive landscape. You will discover how you will gain influence once more in your room and how you can learn to interpret your experiences in an optimistic way. In the chapter after that you'll experience the magic power of luck.

Prosperity

17.
From setback to prosperity

Bad luck: unexpected unpleasant event or condition, adversity, misfortune, disaster, calamity.

Chronic setback can significantly impair your zest for life. If you have to cope with a lot of setbacks you may begin to feel defeated. The forces outside you are stronger than you are, overwhelming. The forces outside you have furnished proof that you have no influence. The ultimate consequence? A mindset in which you expect that calamity is waiting for you 'outside'. From the many depressive people I have been able to coach, I have regularly heard the remark: 'That's me again, see.' This remark illustrates the underlying attitude of the person, a bad-luck attitude. Bad luck is not a trifle because bad luck can slowly but surely change your mindset and associated landscape. The world outside you has slowly but surely become a bad place, you better stay inside. Bad-luck thinking implies not only that you have no influence on the forces outside you, but it also changes your sense of time, because in the expectation that bad events are in store for you, the door of the room and the door to your future will be shut. The powerless darkness is the landscape that remains. But if you have no influence on forces outside you, what do you have influence on? You have influence on the forces inside you! The forces in you bring you back into your dark room and that is exactly where you want to be with your attention, because if you want to shine light you will have to start with yourself. To transform bad-luck thinking I first explain the basics and have you experience how you can gain a sense of influence. In this way you get more control of light and dark in your landscape. In addition, you will learn how to change your mindset so that you don't have to experience your bad luck as a personal attack or failure, but as an event without all that emotional charge. In the following chapter, *Good-luck magnet*, I am going to build on this by changing your bad-luck manner of thinking into the ultimate good-luck attitude: the lucky devil.

> ## 'Everyone has a plan until they get punched in the face.'
> *Mike Tyson*

Bad-luck thinking

'I've had it', says the man in front of me. 'Everything's turning against me, nothing works any more, as if I only have bad luck.' We all have setbacks; it's got to be. We get sick unexpectedly, lose money, a fire breaks out, a loved one dies. But sometimes it seems that you are falling from one accident into another. Sometimes that really is the case. Some people have everything going against them. They lose their jobs, get ill, the contractor goes bankrupt and their partner decides at that moment to chuck it. It happens, unfortunately.

Others also have everything going against them, but in an objective sense not so much happens. Someone cuts you off on the motorway, someone jumps the queue at the checkout, your partner is not listening to you again, you have not slept well again. Seemingly small things that, if you were feeling good, would be insignificant. But sometimes these events are not perceived as a small thing, but as a matter of substantial setback.

In fact, that's what they are, because if you think about it, these are also setbacks but rather setbacks of expectation, of 'how it should be'. Most of us do not want to be cut off by a fellow road user, and if it *does* happen then it may cause a lot of emotions. Why? Because you think it's not supposed to happen, it is contrary to the agreements and 'how we should treat each other'.

> 'I've lived through some terrible
> things in my life, some of
> which actually happened.'
>
> *Mark Twain*

Accidents will happen, but if you suffer a lot of setbacks it may seem there is nothing but adversity in your life. The more setbacks, the more someone can come to experience that things don't go his way only now, but that the chance that they won't go his way again, is rather high. As the setbacks persist, the feeling of adversity shifts to the experience of disaster, the perception that there is an invisible threat waiting to happen as a kind of sinister fate. The world and the people in that world come slowly but surely to be perceived and felt as sources of danger and misery. Misery that you obviously cannot influence any more. Maybe you have never been able to do so.

If the world becomes a place that is against you and the people in that world mean you harm, reject you, don't help you, then it is a lot safer inside.

As the old definitions of depression describe so clearly, it is forces outside us that are larger than ourselves, that we have no defence against and that mean us harm, which is one of the causes of depression. I think there is a lot of truth in that. In our inability to defend ourselves against all these forces, we withdraw more and more mentally and emotionally, so far back that we do not realize that we have ended up in a dark world, one that we can't escape from, but also one where we can't be found by anything that might be against us in the world outside. When adversity has become ordinary and the feeling of impending doom has done its work, a new way of thinking emerges: bad-luck thinking.

People who are seldom lucky (yes, they do exist, let's call them 'bad-luck people' for convenience's sake) appear to share some characteristics:

→ Have a small network because 'it does not matter anyway';

→ Listen badly to their intuition and have fixed goals;

→ Have a future expectation they will be unhappy in and are more susceptible to pessimism, which gives them fewer opportunities;

→ Find it difficult to see the positive side of adversity and to accept it.[64]

Bad-luck thinking is an excellent breeding ground for depression but it is also a symptom of depression in a number of cases. Sometimes it is difficult to determine what was first. When the world outside is an unsafe place, it makes sense to withdraw into the world inside. Bad-luck thinking is an ultimate consequence of adversity, as it ensures that the world becomes an ominous place where you are defeated by forces outside of yourself you were powerless against. The other consequence of that inward movement is that the experience of 'being on your own' is activated or reinforced, as the case may be. Anyway, loneliness and adversity together are the core ingredients of the intensely dismal state. In the deeper conviction that the world means you harm and is an unsafe place where the forces are too big to withstand, with people in that world who mean you harm, don't understand you, use

64 Richard Wiseman, *The Luck Factor; Changing Your Luck, Changing Your Life: the four essential principles*, V.S., 2003

and even abuse you, there is only one way left. The way to hedging in, disconnecting and passivity. Obviously, you have to suffer this fate and you miss the power to keep resisting forces that you know you are not going defeat anyway. You know you won't get what you need. And if even the hope of a miracle has disappeared, only darkness remains. You're defeated.

> 'Loneliness and adversity together are the core ingredients of the intensely dismal state.'

Burnout

There are more and more clues that burnout is accompanied by depression and this isn't that weird. In my experience of guiding clients with burnout problems, I have noticed that there is usually more going on than just an overstrained reaction to (work) pressure. A person rarely has a burnout at work all of a sudden because it has become so busy lately. For instance, in the background a lingering separation is going on in which the partners keep bickering over money and guardianship. The care of the child suffers from this and that gnaws at someone. At work there is a manager who doesn't have any attention for you and always judges you on results that are more and more difficult for you to achieve. Because of the worries you have, your sleep gets increasingly restless and you wake up tired, your new boyfriend turns out to be a huge mistake and your infatuation has turned into daily arguments. You are at the supermarket and can no longer pay with your card... Suddenly you no longer manage to endure all these changes, the light goes out. Your once so resilient spirit is defeated and in survival mode. And when the 'light goes out' we know the kind of gloomy space we end up in.

Sense of influence

In chronic setbacks and depressive complaints, it is important that a sense of control is awakened. I am not talking about forced control but a natural, self-evident, control. The feeling that you are driving your bus instead of your bus being driven by forces outside you. Because if you have no influence left anymore over anything in your world, it is important to have influence over yourself. Viktor Frankl (author of *Man's Search for Meaning*) was aware of this phenomenon. In a world like the concentration camp, where you have no power to decide anymore, where the outside world humiliates you and you have been robbed of everything, there is actually no freedom anymore. There is no freedom left in that world, but there is still freedom in us: the freedom to decide what something means to you.

> 'Even in the most hopeless times I sometimes saw a glimpse of humanity in one of the guards... But it was enough to reassure me... The goodness of man is a flame that can be hidden, but not extinguished.'
>
> *Nelson Mandela*

One example of a person who has used and maintained that freedom is Nelson Mandela. He was detained for 27 years on Robben Island and although he felt he was unjustly locked away and his warders treated him inhumanly, he made a conscious decision. He decided to continue to see his guards as people. As fathers and mothers, sons and daughters, people who work and have a life and a family.[65] Imagine what the difference is when,

---

65 Nelson Mandela, *Long Walk to Freedom: The Autobiography of Nelson Mandela*, 1995

27 years long, you see people around you as monsters or, instead, as people. What happens in you when you look at someone in one way, or in another way? What's the difference?

The big secret of Mandela's decision? The realization that everything can be taken from you but one thing: the freedom to choose what something means to you. That freedom is not in the world around you but is in the world within you. To make the most of that freedom, a sense of control is required, the realization that there is only one person who owns your thoughts. The realization that there is only one person who owns your feelings. The realization that there is only one person who can decide what comes out of your mouth. And the realization that there is only one person who determines how you behave. It is the control that arises from the realization that you are in charge of all these qualities, that they are yours, that you are their owner.

How do you recover a feeling of influence? The feeling of influence and control can be dreadfully far away as you are waiting in the darkness for salvation or a saviour, hoping that something or someone is so kind as to switch the light on for you. Or that, suddenly and magically, a source outside of you will shine light before you, so you can see your path again. That path you were already walking because 'wanting to be happy' was the light outside your room, your sun on the horizon. But you didn't see that light because your room was closed. Perhaps inadvertently, a light outside is precisely what makes you a victim. Why? You have no influence over lights outside yourself and your room. The feeling of being defeated by the outside world and the realization that your salvation is to be found in the outside world is exactly what makes you despondent. There are forces outside you that you have no influence on. It is precisely the external forces that make you dejected. It is precisely the light outside you, whether you call it 'being happy' or 'saviour', which causes you to still yearn for a magical liberation.

What to do? Get influence over the forces in you, because when you come into contact with the forces in you, you can also ignite the light in you. What you really need is for you to take the initiative again, that you find your own way again and that you let the light shine in yourself.

The exercise below *Owning your power* (two parts) lays the foundation for reconnecting with yourself and the forces within yourself. Because if you can't find the light you have to become it.

Owning your power

Part 1
To be able to drive 'your own bus' it is important to realize that we only need to be able to point the way to four elements: our thoughts, our feelings and emotions, our words and our behaviour.

Thoughts:

→ Become aware of your thoughts, the things you think. The ideas you have. The beliefs, all images flashing through your head, your conclusions, judgments, interpretations. Your despondent, negative, gloomy thoughts. Your dissatisfied thoughts, but also your bolstering and supporting thoughts, your optimistic thoughts. Become aware of how you experience your thoughts.

Question:

→ To what extent do you feel that you are the owner of these thoughts? To what extent are you aware that you are creating your thoughts, that no one else creates them than you yourself?

Give a mark:

→ Give yourself a mark for the degree of ownership you are experiencing when you think of your thoughts. 10 = all my thoughts are mine, I decide how I think, 0 = my thoughts happen to me, I don't know how I can influence them, they just happen, they control me.

Draw:

→ Draw a symbol on a piece of paper that symbolizes your thoughts (see the Symbols page at the end of this exercise).

Feelings and emotions:

→ Now become aware of your feelings and emotions, notice how rich or poor your emotional life is. Experience the prevalent emotions and feelings. Become aware of what feelings you find annoying and what are pleasant. Notice which ones you feel too little of and which ones you feel too much of. Experience which feelings are taboo and which you allow.

Question:

→ To what extent do you feel that you are the owner of your feelings and emotions? To what extent are you aware that your feelings and emotions are not just there like that, but that you create them? To what extent do you have emotions that happen to you and to what extent can you give them direction, interrupt, cherish and learn from them?

Give a mark:

→ Give yourself a mark for the degree of ownership you experience when you experience your feelings and emotions. 10 = all my feelings and emotions are mine, 0 = my feelings and emotions happen to me, I don't know how I can influence them, they just happen, they control me.

Draw:

→ Draw a symbol on a piece of paper that symbolizes your feelings and emotions.

Words, speech:

→ Become aware of your breathing, throat, mouth, tongue and voice. Become aware of the extent to which you choose the words you speak. And to what extent you blurt out words. Experience the extent to which you can choose your volume, to what extent you regret the words that have come out of your mouth, to what extent you are aware of the effect of your words? Become aware whether your clam up where you would like to speak, keep silent while you want to speak, whether your throat is blocked or open.

Question:

→ To what extent do you feel that you are the owner of your voice and speech? To what extent are you aware that your words don't just come out of your mouth like that, but that you create them? To what extent do you regret the things you say or, on the contrary, don't say and to what extent can you express yourself, sing, curb yourself?

Give a mark:

→ Give yourself a mark for the degree of ownership of your voice and words you are experiencing. 10 = everything that comes out of my mouth is mine, 0 = my words happen, before I know, I blurt everything out or I clam up completely when I want to speak, I do not know how I can influence them, they control me.

Draw:

→ Draw a symbol on a paper that symbolizes your words and speech.

Behaviour and body:

→ Finally, become aware of your body and your behaviour, the way you behave. Are you happy with your behaviour? Do you do the things you set out to do? Do you leave that bag of chips alone if you have resolved to live healthier or does your arm, before you know it, find itself in a bag of chips? Do you feel that you can control your body, that you can decide how to deal with your body?

Question:

→ To what extent do you feel that you are the owner of your behaviour? To what extent are you aware that your behaviour is not just happening like that, but that you are creating it? To what extent are you quick to lash out, do you hurl rackets or are you sitting in a corner while you actually want to move?

Give a mark:

→ Give yourself a mark for the degree of ownership you are experiencing of your behaviour. 10 = I decide how I behave, what I set out to do, I do, 0 = my behaviour happens to me, my hands and legs lead a life of their own, I do not know how I can influence them, they control me.

Draw:

→ Draw a symbol on a paper that symbolizes your behaviour.

Now take a look at your scores. If you score less than 5 in a category, in all likelihood you often feel helpless. From 5 to 7 there is some ownership and that is probably dependent on stress and adversity. At 8 or higher you drive and control your own bus.

Symbols

The symbol for thoughts

The symbol for sentiments and emotions

The symbol for words and speech

The symbol for behaviour

Owning your power

Part 2
Would you like to feel more ownership of these four inner qualities of yourself? Would you like to experience that you can move in your dark room? Would you like to realize again that you can find the light, can switch it on and even can be it? Would you like to start finding your own way and take initiative? If your answers are yes to these questions then do the following:

Find an item in your house that you feel is yours only. For example, a piece of jewellery of grandma especially for you, a figurine you bought on holiday that you look at daily, a collection, your glasses, your laptop or even your hand. It doesn't matter what it is as long as you can say: 'This is really mine.' Make a list of items, a 'mine'-list:

1.

2.

3.

4.

5.

From this list, take the item you can say about wholeheartedly: 'This is mine.'

Now wonder: How do you know this item is yours? For example, I have a wonderful laptop that I am writing this book on and this laptop is really mine. I also don't want others to work on this laptop. I have chosen it, bought it, paid for it. This laptop is mine. I know that one hundred percent for sure.

How do you know your item is yours?

→ Notice how this feels, what you say to yourself and how you know inside that this item is really yours. The moment you can say wholeheartedly: This is mine, you get the four symbols one by one in front of you. The symbols of your thoughts, feelings and emotions, words and speech, and behaviour.

Now say the following aloud:

→ Say at symbol A - My thoughts are mine.

→ Say at symbol B - My feelings and emotions are mine.

→ Say at symbol C - My voice and words are mine.

→ Say at symbol D - My behaviour is mine.

Repeat this several times. Bring the feeling you have when feeling the ownership of the item, the 'this-is-mine' feeling to the four inner qualities: so, one by one to your thoughts, feelings, voice and behaviour.

Then notice what you are experiencing now. What are you experiencing?

→ Write down:

What difference does this feeling make for you?

→ Write down:

How does this change your experience?

→ Write down:

Imagine you practice this every day the next few weeks.
What would this do for you? Are you going to practice
it? Now make an agreement with yourself on how you're
going to plan this.

It is important to re-discover where your feelings
of influence stem from. You can break through the
disheartening interplay of forces between where you are
in your landscape and where you hope to be. Take the
initiative again, find your own way and let the light shine in
yourself, because if you can't change the world, you have
to change yourself.

Learned helplessness

A budding feeling of influence is absolutely necessary to change your inner landscape. To develop new expectations about how you deal with adversity, you need an additional quality: optimism. In order to build a new happiness molecule and experience zest for life, it is important that you are able to mould pessimism into optimism. The seed of optimism causes you to develop a different relationship with what is going to come on your path, especially with the setbacks that will come on your path.

> 'Optimist: Someone who figures that taking a step backward after taking a step forward is not a disaster, it's more like a cha-cha-cha.'
>
> *Robert Brault*

Martin Seligman, in his best-seller *Learned Optimism* (1991), has described in detail what the characteristics of a pessimistic and optimistic mindset are. It is important to realize that optimism and pessimism are not character traits. Pessimism and optimism are evaluation styles, ways of evaluating an experience. Individuals with a pessimistic evaluation style assess setbacks quite differently than is done by individuals with an optimistic evaluation style. So, you haven't got a pessimistic character but you have learned to evaluate in a pessimistic manner and what you have learnt you can change. Seligman speaks of 'learned helplessness' to explain the pessimistic mindset. Learned helplessness is helplessness, which, as the word says, has been learned. So you weren't born with it, but your environment and your reaction patterns to setbacks have taught you to what extent you can affect events outside yourself. Once you experience that you have no or little influence on events, you could call that helplessness. In this light, one could say that pessimism is in line with depression. That is true. However, pessimism in itself does not necessarily lead to a 'dark room'. Evaluating or assessing pessimistically is only one of the contributing factors in the development of depression. Just as well as optimism is not the happiness molecule, but only one of the factors contributing to it.

A lesson in pessimism

Now sit back and relax, we're going to do a lesson in pessimism. When I picked up the idea to write a book about happiness and depression the first thing I did was model pessimism. I wondered if people with a depressive streak have a corresponding pessimistic strategy, and was curious about when pessimism turns into depression. Pessimism is really easy to learn if you do your best...

SANDRA

Sandra tried hard to complete a work project and after a weekend of working nonstop she was able to finish it by the skin of her teeth. Tired but satisfied she goes to her work the next day to present it. Everyone listens attentively and when the end of the presentation approaches, she feels relieved. Overall, everyone is satisfied, but her manager talks to her alone.

'You've given a nice presentation and hit the nail on the head with those figures you presented. I just missed the action steps, because I think we had agreed that you would include them in your presentation as well'.

The ground is washing away from under her feet; somehow, this hits home.

'What a mistake!' She feels she is getting small and would like to hide.

'How stupid I am', she thinks but from her mouth only excuses emanate.

That day she walks around at work with a rotten feeling and it seems like her colleagues are talking about her behind her back. Behind all the smiling faces Sandra sees glances of 'that one is stupid' and she begins to behave accordingly. When she comes home at night, her boyfriend is waiting for her. She would like to fall into his arms to tell him how rotten she feels, but she laughs

CHAPTER 17 > **FROM SETBACK TO PROSPERITY**

and acts as if nothing is the matter. She tries to open a bottle of wine with the new corkscrew and somehow does not succeed. Her boyfriend sees her messing around and says: 'Just let me do it.' Instead of appreciating his offer as a helping hand, she snarls: 'I'm not crazy or anything, you know, I really can do something.' He answers: 'Give me a break, girl, what's the matter with you?' The rest of the evening they chat about this and that, but Sandra's head is haunted by memories of previous mistakes she has made, and there are very many of them in her experience. The next day she has to go to work, but she is not looking forward one little bit to those judging colleagues. With a knot in her stomach she drives to the office. Sandra tries to avoid her colleagues. Her manager asks her if she wants to think along with a new marketing plan, but Sandra only mentions objections and why she has no time to occupy herself with it. As time passes, she sees increasingly often trouble ahead, actually she had always been a bit like that...

What has happened here? As said, it is easy to develop a pessimistic evaluation style. Actually, you only have to do three things:

→ *Make the setback personal.* In the case of Sandra: She sees the feedback of her manager in relation to her person. Instead of labelling the setback as an error, or as a snapshot, she sees the setback in relation to her person. How dumb I am, she thinks.

→ *Transfer the setback to other contexts.* She takes her feelings of failure along to her private situation and thinks that there, too, she is not the smartest either.

→ *Begin to fantasize about potential problems in the future with this problem.* As befits an effective pessimist, she takes the setback along to the future that hasn't hitherto taken place. She starts to avoid situations and is already throwing up roadblocks.

A pessimist is an excellent generalizer. An isolated experience is generalized and spread like creamy butter. For example, the manager's feedback is 'spread out' towards her identity and the work experience is taken along to her private situation. Eventually, she even spreads the experience already into her possible future. Yes, a pessimist is good at generalizing.

An optimistic mindset
Even if things aren't going your way

When you think optimistically about events and people that are going against you, your expectation for the future changes for the better. Pessimism ensures that you have a negative expectation for the future and in particular see bumps in the road ahead. If you see a negative event through optimistic glasses, you do not assess the setback as something about you as a person, but as something outside your personality. It is the mental and emotional ability to continue to consider a setback as an occasion to learn, develop and above all an instance of your behaviour rather than who you are. It is the realization that you are doing things that may be wrong and that others are doing things that may be tedious and negative, but that these are and remain matters of your behaviour. In addition, optimism is the ability to keep the same event linked to the situation of the setback. So if a contractor takes you in, the check-out girl is not taking you in straight away when she short-changes you. No, you keep the setback in the context where it took place. Finally, optimism is the ability to keep an event fixed in time. Instead of doing a scan past all the previous experiences and fantasizing about all the future experiences that might go wrong, the optimist knows how to keep a negative experience where it happened: 'there', 'then', instead of: 'you see, that's me again, soon things will go wrong again...'

Interpreting setbacks as an optimist

Doing instead of being. Link the adversity to behaviour rather than to your personality.

Keep the setback only linked to the situation where it occurred instead of finding evidence that you fail in other situations too.

Keep the setback small by linking it to that one moment of the day instead of looking for evidence of previous moments of failure and expecting you will fail again.

'Pessimists are right but optimists have more fun.'

Lucas Derks

How do you learn to think more like an optimist?

Learning to think like an optimist requires some discipline for a while. You have probably cultivated your pessimistic evaluation style for years and brought to a high level of efficiency. I suspect that, if you have done your very best, you can quickly lapse into a pessimistic mood at the smallest setback. In this mood you may react emotionally, negatively and insecurely as to the near future. Because your evaluation style is so perfected, some attention and time are needed to start actively evaluating in an optimistic manner.

Where pessimists are good at generalizing, optimists are good at specifying. It looks like optimists perceive more accurately. As if they look better at the facts, at what exactly happens, and thus are able to keep events more in the moment, more in the events themselves.

Stopping pessimism!

Some time ago a client told me he has an odd response when the phone rings. When he is called by a number he does not recognize, he refuses to answer the phone. He also feels instantly insecure when that happens and then immediately imagines the most negative scenario. He then looks for the phone number on the internet and if he discovers who it is, and it is not a person or organization that gives him 'problems' as he calls it, he calls back. In his head, as quick as lightning a film plays in which it is clear that he comes off worst and he will probably have 'blundered'. A special reaction process, as you also may notice yourself. He has no idea who is calling and what about, but he is so terrified of the possible problematic situation that might arise that he has only one option: not to answer the phone. Is this an exceptional situation? No, this occurs in a variety of ways and with many people, much more than you would expect.

How can Sandra now ensure that she stops evaluating pessimistically in similar situations? What else can she do with the same information? What is needed to get a more optimistic view of the same situation?

Creating optimistic thoughts

With this exercise you carry on building a high-spirited landscape. From the feeling of influence of the previous process, you can also influence how you learn to interpret events. Because if you don't interpret setbacks that negatively you have less reason to withdraw and that can be the beginning of finding a real opening. Look upon the process described below as a ritual, a process where every time a setback occurs, you get the chance to view it in a different light.

1. Now concentrate on your shoe or something else you're wearing, that is 'enveloping you'.

2. Ask yourself the following question: 'Are you your shoe?' Take a moment to let the question sink in: 'Am I my shoe?' You should say no because your shoe is around you and is not part of you, and also because your shoe cannot move on its own and you, on the contrary, can move your foot. Moreover, you say no because your shoe has no feeling and you have. You can step

out of your shoe, but not out of yourself; and so on. Become increasingly more aware that you are not your shoe. At the very most you 'have' your shoe, but you're not it. Agree?

3. Be aware of the distinction between you and your shoe, the dividing line between the two of you. The difference between what you are and what you are not. Keep that feeling with you.

4 Remember a moment when something nasty was happening to you and you reacted to it pessimistically. Call that event to mind.

→ Notice inside how you are making the event personal and how you are seeing it in relation to who you are.

→ Also, notice how you are bringing this event into the future by creating negative future expectations and how you are evoking similar memories that intensify your sense of pessimism.

→ Also experience how you take the event to other contexts and situations.

→ How are you feeling?

5. Now imagine that you can see the same situation in front of you, as if you were watching a movie and can see yourself in that situation and what is happening there.

6. Keep the feeling between you and your shoe (I'm not my shoe) clear and look with that feeling at yourself as in a film, and what happens there. Answer the following questions:

→ 'What exactly is happening there?' Don't be tempted into generalities, no, be precise. Repeat this question until you have an accurate picture of what actually happened. 'What exactly is the other doing?' 'What exactly am I doing?'

→ While you continue to experience that you are not your shoe, say the following phrases aloud (or in yourself if you are in a public situation):

- 'What happened there, says nothing about who I am, it says something about what I do.' Repeat this sentence until you begin to experience its significance.
- 'What happened there only happens in that situation.' Repeat this sentence until you begin to experience its significance.
- 'What happened there is something from then and not now.' Repeat this sentence until you begin to experience its significance.
- Say aloud: 'That I am not, that happens there, that happened then.'

→ Notice how this feels and what you are experiencing now when you think of that nasty experience. Also notice how your feeling about yourself changes, how your feeling about the future changes.

→ Experience how this affects your sense of pessimism.

→ Ask yourself: 'Do I want to feel like this, with a budding optimism about this experience, or rather pessimistic, the way I felt before?'

→ If your answer is 'yes' to the first question and 'no' to the second, then practice this in all situations where you are tempted to evaluate things on the pessimistic side.[66]

Summary

How do you get a feeling of influence back when you are feeling helpless? What are you able to influence when all kinds of things happen you have no control over? The answer is as simple as complex, because if you can't change your circumstances it's time to change yourself. Changing yourself begins with the question of what you do have an influence on. By practicing how you can own your powers, you get the initiative again, which is exactly what you need. Once you boost again the awareness that you are the owner of your thoughts, feelings, speech and behaviour,

66 See my videoblog *Helpless to optimism* on Wassilizafiris.nl

you can begin to decide how you interpret your life experiences. We cannot completely bypass setbacks, but we can certainly change the way we experience adversity. By experiencing your influence on yourself, you become the owner of your inner landscape and that brings zest for life one more step closer.

Coincidence

18.
Good-luck magnet

Constant and chronic setback results in at least one thing: it ensures that your expectation of the future changes. Depression has taught me that in the mind of a depressed person 'happiness' no longer exists at all. It has become a meaningless concept. So much so that there is no longer any active pursuit of happiness, and when it is completely dark, the desire to be happy may also disappear. As if it doesn't exist anymore and as if it doesn't exist anymore in the inner landscape of the person either. 'Being happy' is a light that is so far away and has proved so unachievable that it has been given up. Bad-luck thinking affects us greatly, it strengthens the feeling that happiness is no longer in store for you, and thus changes your inner perspective. Your inner world is shrinking and the world beyond becomes progressively elusive and threatening.

In this chapter I explain in more depth how setbacks can lead to a bad-luck mindset and what the consequences of that are. I also tell you how expectations and happiness are coupled together by the 'happiness formula', but the most important thing is that I take you along to the world of the 'good-luck magnet', because if you become familiar with that landscape the light will shine in you again.

Unlucky guy

If you experience setback after setback, your future perspective changes unwittingly. Slowly but surely you start to expect that even more calamity is waiting for you. There is the expectation of adversity, as if the world is not for you, as if you were the unlucky bird that has just come off worst. All others do have that bit of luck, but you don't.

If you lose the feeling that things are coming 'your way' then you lose your inner future perspective. Our future perspective is, all things considered, not at all in the real world, but exists only in our inner world. The realization that there is a tomorrow and a day after tomorrow, and even a next year, can incite us to great deeds. We start a family with the expectation that we'll stay together forever, invest everything we have and start a business because we believe that there will be a fruitful future for it in store, we build a house with the idea to be able to enjoy it over the next thirty years.

But none of these expectations are associated with any established truth. We do these things in the expectation that we will live to see it. However, what if those inner future projections disappear? What if your future stops... now? What if our inner 'future timeline' disappears in a sea of adversity? Suppose there is so much real or felt adversity in you that you cannot but expect that adversity lies in wait for you and that your future is interspersed by more of the same, a future that is not worth living. A future that you'd rather stay away from than go towards. Imagine that your future disappears and nothing else remains than a present, a present without meaningful bonds, a present you are not welcome in...

If happiness has disappeared from your experience, there is not much else left than a sad, lonely existence. Depressed individuals don't try anymore to find happiness at all, because it is too big and too far away, offers too much resistance. Too many things in life prove the opposite of it, it seems totally impossible. Useless too. But one thing still resonates, or, as one of my clients told me: 'What if luck would come my way a bit?' This seems to be a futile remark, but in the context of this whole narrative it is not.

From good-luck thinking to lucky guy

The English scientist and writer Richard Wiseman invites a number of people to an interview and just before the person arrives, he puts a five-pound note on the pavement in front of the café where they agreed to meet. To his surprise, the people who describe themselves as lucky persons see the note and snatch it up, but the unlucky persons all leave the money where it is. Why? They simply aren't seeing it. At the end of the interview, the researcher asked if there were any other things that had caught the eye during or before the interview. Some of the participants indicated that they had found money and believed that this was their 'lucky day'. To the researcher's great surprise, each one who had called himself a lucky guy had found the money, while none of the 'unlucky guys' had found the money.[67]

'We all tend to feel good
when things go our way;
we feel we are generally
winning in the game of life.'

From: *Should grief be treated like depression*?
Dr. Charles Raison CNN February 17, 2012

When I read that, a door opened. What if it were the case that lucky guys have more good luck in life because they perceive themselves that way, and that unlucky guys have no luck because they perceive themselves as unlucky guys? Could it be that a lucky guy has more good luck purely because he or she looks at the world differently?

Good-luck formula
Seven years after my proverbial door opened and my research was already in a concluding phase, the article *This is the equation for happiness* was published in Time Magazine Online in August 2014. In the article a mathematical formula was cited. A mathematical formula that specifies

67 Steve Andreas, *Becoming Lucky*, 2008

the ingredients of happiness and not just a 'chance' formula, a formula that was tested on eighteen thousand participants. This study looked at how financial rewards affected the feeling of happiness and, as expected, showed that winning or losing money affects our sense of happiness. One of the premises in that study was that 'expectations affect the experience of happiness'. A premise that we all know already and which has been mentioned several times in this book (chapter 2, *Emotions and a happy life*). When you have high expectations and those expectations don't come true, it affects your state of mind negatively. You feel disappointed. The researchers discovered that expectations are a very precise yardstick for the sense of happiness. But that our moods can be so strongly influenced by the events of life surprised the investigators. The relationship between having expectations and whether or not experiencing feelings of happiness proved so consistent that they could sum it up in a formula:

$$\text{Happiness}(t) = w_0 + w_1 \sum_{j=1}^{t} \gamma^{t-j} CR_j + w_2 \sum_{j=1}^{t} \gamma^{t-j} EV_j + w_3 \sum_{j=1}^{t} \gamma^{t-j} RPE_j,$$

Put more simply: Happiness is your basic average mood +how much loss you can accept (CR) + what you win on average when you gamble (EV) + the difference with what you actually get (RPE).[68]

But surely you have no influence on whether luck is on your side, or enjoy prosperity, a pleasant surprise or a windfall? That would be the same as thinking that when as a lucky guy you buy a lottery ticket you will definitely win the prize. Then let the millions flow in... No, that's not the same. Hoping you win the lottery has little to do with

---

68 Alexandra Sifferlin, *This is the Equation for Happiness*, Times.com, 4 August 2014

happiness. Because if this expectation doesn't come true, your happiness experience will decrease, and, what's more, you won't have any influence on the lottery. But what if you do gain influence on whether you're lucky or not?

That's me again, what a stroke of luck

The trickiest beliefs that people can develop are negating beliefs that limit what is possible for a person. People who believe they are 'unlucky guys' believe that they have 'no luck', 'only bad things happen to me'. Many people who face setbacks develop negative beliefs such as 'I am out of luck'. I had that kind of belief myself, too. I even remember that I said that literally. One setback after the other piled up with me. Sitting in my house under construction, looking at the mess that didn't seemed to lessen, this feeling took me by surprise. 'My luck has definitely run out.' Discouragement and hopelessness had taken possession of me. In some sort of automatism, I was dragging shelves from left to right. I didn't dare to think about tomorrow because the only thing that tomorrow was to bring was more of the same, even more bad luck. Later I noticed that my depressive clients said this in similar terms.

Richard Wiseman has interviewed people who labelled themselves as 'unlucky' (in the sense of having bad luck) and 'lucky' (in the sense of lucky guy). He lays down four principles that seem to be true for the 'lucky ones' among us:

1. Lucky guys increase their possibilities by a large network of friends. They tell their friends about their wishes and dreams, who, in their turn, talk about them with others. This greatly increases the chances of the dream or desire being realised.
2. They listen to premonitions and intuition and are open to pursue other avenues to achieve their goals.

3. They expect to be lucky in the future which helps them to cope with and get over repeated setbacks.
4. They see the positive side of adversity.

'Diligence is the mother of good luck.'

Benjamin Franklin

So, people who tag themselves as lucky actually have better luck than people who don't see themselves as such. And that's just the beginning, because believing that you're a lucky guy, makes you feel as one, and that's a huge advantage. Because feeling lucky does not change the world around us straight away, but it certainly changes the world in us. That will make you more aware of the real opportunities in the world. Moreover, you are a pleasanter person to be with. Consequently, you attract more people, and more people lead to more possibilities and opportunities.

Feeling like a lucky guy makes that all experiences can become opportunities. Thus, even initially unpleasant experiences such as missing the train to an important appointment can be an opportunity. For you met an interesting new person in the hectic situation because you had to ask when the next train would go. When you feel lucky, you are more inclined to take an initiative like asking someone for help rather than keep trying for hours yourself. The benefit of that can be strong. Good luck happens to you in a number of cases but more often it requires initiative, and initiative is actually one of the things that are in your power. So, the more initiative the more likely you meet people who can help you.

Because you believe that you are a lucky guy, you are much more tenacious in adversity and are even willing to try out even seemingly impossible situations. And good-luck believers even go as far as to interpret the biggest setback like a terminal disease as an opportunity: only now do I understand how to live meaningfully, for example. The things of life that you take 'for granted' are suddenly not that commonplace anymore, but gifts. The smallest things can then get significant. The appreciation you can then feel is a great and exciting force. When you begin to think in that vein, you increasingly attract experiences that prove how good the world is for you. You become, as it were, a good-luck magnet, a person who expects good luck because that's the way it is. Your future is a place that pulls at you, the world a place to discover, people become opportunities instead of threats, life a fertile place, a place you go for.

As a good-luck guy you can distinguish three types of luck:

1. Pure luck.
   We all have had a bit of luck once. The time you found five euros. A little bit of luck. Finding a fiver is clearly a bit of luck. For example, you can also experience it as a piece of luck when all of a sudden you find the shoes you like so much in the sale. Or in the street you find a screw that you happen to need. 'Just my luck!' you'll often think then. You can also call it 'pure luck'.

2. Unexpected luck.
   There are also more unexpected forms of luck. The luck that you were just at the right time in the right place. For example, that party where, in hindsight, you met your new love, or that friend who introduced you to someone who happened to know someone who turned out to need your expertise, and that in this way you have come by your new job. 'Just my luck!' That you were just on the right spot for something. Or that the insurance paid you out more than expected. Or that someone brought your lost wallet back to you. For example, I once left my credit card in the ATM in a foreign country and discovered this weeks later. I called

my bank and nothing turned out to be debited. What unexpected luck!

3. Unlikely luck.
   Unlikely luck is luck that at first glance you don't consider luck at all. At first, an event or experience can seem very negative but if you look at it in a different way... you see a luck of a different order: you felt in time that your rear wheel wasn't fixed properly on your car and that you stopped in time on the hard shoulder. Or that accident on the road that happened just after you. Situations that you escaped an accident by a hair's breadth, or that you turned out not to be ill after all. Maybe even traumas that with hindsight appear to have been godsends. For example, my daughter once crossed the road and I had seen the approaching car too late. The car missed her by an inch. What luck! These events are negative, but because you have escaped a negative consequence it is 'unlikely luck'.

Isn't it time to awaken the lucky guy in you, the lucky devil? Isn't it time to step through the opening of the door into a world full of opportunities? Then do the 'Good-luck magnet' and change your future expectations.

Good-luck magnet

1. Make a list of pure good-luck experiences. Go back in time, maybe even long ago. If necessary, take a few weeks over this list but write down all the experiences that you consider to be pure luck in your life. Don't leave out anything, even if you only found a pound or a dollar or just that tiny screw in the street you had been looking for quite some time.
   Write down:

2. Create a list of unexpected forms of luck you've experienced. Events that initially don't look like good-luck, but after all appear to belong in the category of unexpected luck.
   Write down:

3. Create a list of events that are (extremely) negative or may have been negative in your life, which you can describe (in hindsight) as unlikely good-luck events.
   Write down:

Now look at your good-luck list and get back every memory one by one:

4. Start with a memory of good-luck, pure luck.

5. When you have one such memory, experience for a moment how it feels. And proceeding from that feeling you remember another moment of a little bit of luck. From that feeling you remember another time. Recall five or six memories and collect them as it were in your mind and make some kind of collage in your head of good-luck experiences.

6. Then go to memories of unexpected luck. Repeat the process above and group all these events together in your mind. As if you have a growing collage in your head composed of unexpected luck experiences.

7. Then good-luck moments of another order, unlikely luck. Do the same as above and expand your luck collage.

Take a moment to see that whole luck collage mentally in front of you.

8. Enjoy all that happiness that has fallen to you, feel how it feels to have experienced so much good-luck in your life and repeat the words 'Just my luck'. Let these words form a framework in which you realize how much luck you have in your life and let all associations spontaneously emerge from even more moments and events of luck. 'That's me again, even more good luck.' Replace the phrase 'That's me again, even more bad luck', with 'That's me again, even more good luck'.

Enjoy this feeling of good luck and how the world can be a good-luck place, how people can be with you in a good-luck pact, how life is full of opportunities, possibilities and luck. Do you realize how much luck you have had and, therefore, how much luck is in store for you?! If you have already had so much luck so far, then,

inevitably, many situations will crop up that appear to be good luck in all sorts of unexpected ways...

→ Imagine keeping this way of thinking about the things that happen in your life with you, what difference will this make for you?

→ How does this change your inner landscape? What has happened in your inner landscape? Is the door ajar?

→ Take the time to explore your inner landscape.

Notice in the coming weeks how your view on the world can change now that you know how many opportunities are hidden in your everyday experiences. Put your luck glasses on and take the time to let your luck collage grow and grow in the coming weeks and months so that the light can become bigger and brighter...

Inner landscape

I have talked a lot about the inner landscape and especially your inner landscape. Now is the time to make your landscape a little more literal.

Grasp what you have been exploring so far. At the beginning of this part you have acquired a clearer picture of your starting position, the state of mind you were in when you embarked on part 3. Perhaps you were already aware of the landscape you were in, maybe you were already aware of how dark that world was and how shut off you were from the world outside your world.

Now we are seven steps further. You have worked on connection by feeling acknowledged and accepted again, making closeness more natural and you have been given tips to take a more vulnerable stance. That, too, is essential for connection. You have updated your self-image so you could become whole again, connected with yourself.

Moreover, you have been working on a new belief about yourself so that you can realize that you are good as you are and valuable, and in the eyes of others as well. You have experienced what you can influence and how you can own your powers and how you can interpret experiences optimistically. Finally, you have converted your bad-luck thinking into a good-luck mindset. You have experienced significant changes step by step.

Become aware of how all these steps have changed your inner landscape. How has your inner landscape changed?

Answer this question by drawing your landscape.

Draw your inner landscape

On the next page you see a puppet, that's you. You are in the midst of your landscape. Answer the following questions and draw the answers at the right spot in the landscape.

1   How do these seven steps change your inner landscape?

→ Answer:

2. How does this change your experience?

→ Answer:

3. What's in front of you (in your mind)? This can be anything from a meadow, to forests, to a city, to the sea and so on.

→ Draw this in front of the puppet.

4. What's on your left (literally directly on your left)? This can be anything from a meadow, to forests, to a city, to the sea and so on.

→ Draw this on the puppet's left.

5. What's on your right (literally directly on your right)? This can be anything from a meadow, to forests, to a city, to the sea and so on.

→ Draw this on the puppet's right.

6 What's behind you (literally behind you)? This can be anything from a meadow, to forests, to a city, to the sea and so on.

→ Draw this behind the puppet.

Trust in what emerges in you.

7. Now that you know what is in front of you, at your left, at your right and behind you, what do you experience?

→ And how does this change your experience?

A new inner landscape makes you move differently in your outward landscape. You can find other and even new meanings in the landscapes you are active in. With a new inner landscape, the same experiences, events and people may gain a different meaning and so may be experienced differently by you. Keep your new landscape in sight over the coming weeks. You don't have to actively tinker in it or change things. All you have to do is keep your new landscape in your consciousness. Find out what that does for you. That simple? Yes, that simple.

Joyful

What else? Now is the time to shape the world you live in and prepare your mindset for a life full of opportunities and fulfilment. It is about time to enter your future and not only to attract good fortune as a lucky guy but also to shape your future concretely.

A part of the zest-for-life gestalt is joy. That does not have to be a continual 'happy peppy' state of mind, because happiness and zest for life require constant attention, just like gardening. Once your inner landscape has changed, it does not alter the fact that in our external landscape there are always challenges that call for maintenance. Joy is a part of zest for life that you can definitely have an effect on if you keep up and maintain what makes you happy. In the exercise below you get handles to make your new landscape and the world you live in joyful and pleasant.

Living joyfully
What makes you cheerful?

1. Make a list of all the normal things that cheer you up. Think of everyday, ordinary things: a good cup of coffee in the morning at your favourite café. Playing with the dog or your child. Reading a good book.

2. Now check which items from the list are easy to carry out and create a plan for them. If reading a book gives you joy, for example, and you realize that you can easily plan it, make a plan for how often and at what times you like to do it.

3. Investigate which items in the list are difficult to achieve and examine what stops you from realising them.

→ Which of the examples you mentioned of what makes you joyfull are hard to achieve for you?

→ What stands in the way of integrating these things into your daily life?

4. Then choose the top three essential items (from both lists together) that matter to you for a happy life.

1.

2.

3.

Go and do these things. Or find a way to be able to do them. Remind yourself daily of what you really want: To make yourself joyful, cheerful.

5. Adjust this every three months, go along your list once more and take stock of which of all these items have already been accomplished and which still need to be accomplished.

Summary

Bad-luck thinking arises because you lose your future perspective by repeated setbacks. That will make you close your inner landscape and then you expect more of the same, even more bad luck. However, the door can open outward again, light can shine through the door's crack or light dots can be visible in your inner landscape so that you have a landmark again. Your experience of bad luck may change. For that, it is important to remember that you want to experience again how it is to be lucky. Being lucky creates a wondrous experience, it opens the way to the future, hence the Good-luck magnet is so crucial for you. You have rounded off your zest-for-life gestalt with the latest quality, joy. Joy is not just something that happens to us. We experience joy because we do things that cheer us up, make us happy. And these things can be done daily or weekly. In the last chapter (chapter 19) *Universal motives* I take you along to show you how you create perspective in your future. As said before, I have always advised against setting targets when you are still in a dark room. Goals can be of added value when your landscape permits. In Universal motives I am going teach you a new way of setting targets, one that is very close to your natural motives. That's why I call them Natural goals.

Seeing
the Light

19.
Universal motives

Although our lives are changing, our inner landscapes can remain static. We already know that this is the case because patterns repeat themselves. Our patterns repeat themselves because we set our goals from the rules that our inner landscape has drawn up for us. That is why we run constantly into the same barriers, our efforts continue to result in the same results and we are constantly seeking out the same kind of people in our lives. In the happiness culture we live in, the extent to which our lives can be shaped is central. Only, how makeable is your life when your inner landscape is immutably fixed? To change your life, it is therefore important to get to know your landscape so that it can become clear where you are. Setting goals about health, fitness, career, relationship, money, happiness and life are (however temporarily attractive) ultimately useless and even problem reaffirming if your starting point is not clear. In deconstructing the depression gestalt and when building the zest-for-life gestalt something magical happens: instead of having to create goals, the goals announce themselves. That means that goals are revealed to you in the new landscape and chances are that these are goals that you could not have imagined beforehand. If you actually think about it, that makes sense, because a landscape that you don't know yet creates opportunities that you have not experienced yet.

In this last chapter, I'll take you into your future. An exploration of your new landscape, the landscape you live your life in every day. The landscape of your relationships, family ties, study, career, love, health, money, spirituality, you name it. To live your life with enthusiasm, you need a healthy relationship with yourself, one in which you are connected with yourself, with others and with the world around you. We are going to set goals now... but now in a different way than most of you are accustomed to.

The rest of your life...

Living your life well in the moment is a great experience. And although the 'now' is the place to be, the 'now' is only a fine place if your perception of what is to come is also fine. The Good-luck magnet technique has helped you to see your world and the people in that world again as a place with opportunities, where people offer opportunities and not only obstructions. Now that light shines anew in your world, the awareness of a future full of desire can slowly emerge in you. If you feel free to choose your direction and explore how your path runs, you can come back into contact with your inner motives, your incentives. In my other book *IK BEN niet alleen op de wereld* (English edition: *Meaningful Profit*) I have described three universal motives that are motives for all of us. I have found that if you integrate these deep motives into your desire, your desire is not going to stay a desire, but is going to be a goal that must be achieved. A goal, of course, you want to achieve.

Our three natural motives are: autonomy, mastery and meaning. Each of these motives has its own motivational strength and motivation duration. They seem to be innate motivation sources and the more we draw on them the greater the chance that we can make our desires 'naturally' turn into reality.

Ensuring that you integrate these three natural motives (autonomy, mastery, meaning) into your desires not only helps you to be closer to your own nature, but you also feel more passionate, more powerful and more cheerful.

Autonomy

The desire to be able to influence your world as a self-reliant person is a basic motivation that we all have and is linked to our experience of self-government, security and certainty. We need safety on a daily basis. As soon as we are not safe, we experience it as a deficit, and that is such a threat that we will do everything we can to make good that deficit, until the sense of security is restored. Deficiency needs are tremendously strong forces because all our attention goes to satisfying the need, but once it is satisfied, the need has disappeared and we have almost forgotten that we were looking for security at all. A deficiency need therefore creates a *lot of motivational strength but short motivational duration.* One of the most important forms of expression of this motive is the desire to exert influence, the sense of control, so that you are not subject to forces outside yourself that can cause a deficit. You can observe this need very well among growing children. 'I can do it myself', who doesn't know that little sentence? And as soon as the little one can cope, exploration is extended to what else is possible.

Mastery

Mastery is the need to do what we do, well. This is not the same as perfectionism, but it is the desire to excel in the capabilities available to us, our best 'I', so to speak. Everyone has natural curiosities which are just there. For example, you see that in children natural curiosities manifest themselves, which they naturally pay a lot of attention to and equally naturally get and want to get better and better at. It almost seems (and maybe it is) a biological need, to explore to the limit what you have in you, to expand your possibilities, stretching them over and over again. That expectation to be 'better' and 'more proficient' is one that can induce great pleasure and joy. An example of a natural curiosity? I used to take apart all the radios at home, to my mother's great frustration because I failed at putting them back together. But why did I do that? I wanted to know where the sound came from. If you think about it, it is still my greatest passion because to really help people I have to understand 'where the sound comes from'. You can recognize your own natural curiosities by the things that you can unfailingly be warmed up to, throughout your life. Experiences you say yes to whenever possible. These are experiences that, as it were, have your name all over them, and are driven by a great inquisitiveness and a great longing for more and better.

Meaningfulness

Meaningfulness is a great but trickier motivator for the simple reason that this is not a deficiency need but an existential need and existential needs are initially weak in motivational force. Once we appear to be able to flesh out our sense of meaning, our motivation increases rather than diminishes. *The motivational strength and duration increase as you become better at achieving what is meaningful to you.* Meaningfulness is perhaps less woolly than you might think. Many parents recognize the feeling of meaning when it comes to their children. Your children are your most tangible legacy and parents want their children to do as well as possible. Many adults even experience a sense of meaningfulness for the first time when children come into their lives.

To bring the three natural motives and your desires together requires some attention. In the process described below, you undertake a natural exploration of your future, the future of the rest of your life.

Natural targets

1. Ask yourself the following question:

→ Now that I have arrived at this point in my life, what do I want with the rest of my life?[69] Answer this question in the context of this book in relation to good luck, happiness and/or dejection.

→ What do you want (do) with the rest of your life?
Write down:

Have there been positive things in your life so far that have helped you to achieve the future that you describe in 1. Ask yourself:

→ Which positive aspects of your present life do you want to take along with you into your ideal future (from 1)?
Write down:

Of course, there are issues, ways of doing, thoughts, beliefs and experiences that you want to banish and not take with you into your desired future.

69 If you want to enjoy your new landscape and don't want to look at the future right now, that's fine too. Take a few weeks and do this exercise then. You have plenty of time.

→ What matters, events, feelings, thoughts, beliefs should you eliminate in order to be able to enter that future? Write down:

2. Imagine you'll manage to live this future completely.

Ask yourself:

→ What will this mean to you?
Answer:

→ And what will... (The answer to the previous question) do for you?
Answer:

→ And what will... (The answer to the previous question) do for you?
Answer:

→ And what will... (The answer to the previous question) do for you?
Answer:

Take a moment to realize what accomplishing this will do for you and how relevant this is for you. Notice what this is doing with your motivation.

3. What natural curiosity you may have had from childhood, can you link to this desire? What natural curiosity is being fuelled and satisfied with this goal?
   Answer:

Enjoy this for a moment.

4. Imagine that you have already completely realized this future. Next year you'll be living this future. You are sitting on the couch and your most important loved one(s) is or are sitting next to you on the couch. Imagine, for example, that your children are sitting beside you on the couch, next to a father or mother who has brought these changes into his or her life. A changed person. Please note: If you don't have or want children, fantasize that this is the case. If that's very difficult for you, remember that the most important person in your life is sitting next to you.

5. Just imagine that you step into your child's shoes and take place (as your child) next to a father or mother who has brought about this change in his or her life. Notice how it is to sit next to this father/mother who has changed so much. Experience how it is and how it feels to sit next to this father/mother.
   Ask yourself the following question:

→ What does it give me (as a child) to sit next to this father or mother who has realized this future?
Answer:

→ What more does it give me? What do I get now from my father/
mother that I want to take along the rest of my life?
Answer:

Step back into yourself.

6. Now when you think of the rest of your life: How motivated are
   you to achieve that future?

→ Give yourself a mark on a scale from 0 to 10
(0 = no motivation, 10 = all the motivation you can think of).
Mark:

7. Now ask yourself what the tiniest thing is you can do daily to
   make this future a reality.

Setting goals in connection with your natural motives
strengthens desire and increases your resilience. Because
in everyday life there are again and again things or people
or just our own thoughts and feelings that can make us
drop our desires. As soon as you have connected your
wishes to your deepest motives, it is not only natural to
realize your wishes but also to experience the motivation
to continue, even if there are things going wrong.

Summary

We function well when we live in a satisfied 'now'. The now becomes even more beautiful when we realize that there is a future waiting for us that corresponds to the possibilities of our inner landscape. Seeing your desires realized can give a lot of joy in life. The ability to match your natural motives to the desires you have will make your natural motivation connect to the things that are so essential to you. This motivation helps you to realize why it is important to achieve your desires and helps you to persevere where before you might have pulled out. Natural objectives give you meaning, perseverance and resilience.

Happiness
is like
Gardening.
It requires
constant
attention

Conclusion

The road to zest for life that you have walked now, I have walked myself, too. Although I didn't know at the time what steps I was making. As you know from *My story*, I was also quite wiped out when Elize came to visit me and John became my client. Without being aware of it, they have helped me tremendously in my own transformation process. John, because I wanted to understand his dejection, and Elize, because she invited me to go on holiday for a week. In that holiday my first penny dropped after which many were still to follow.

Elize proposed to go to Spain for a week. Her proposal completely dropped out of the sky for me, and I replied: 'I'll go with you if you like, but don't expect anything from me.' I had not discussed with her how I felt, but that was obviously not necessary either. 'Good', she said. 'I'll organize it.'

Before I knew it, we were in a cottage on the island of La Gomera in Spain. The way we spent our days consisted of a few basic things: breakfast, a cup of coffee by the beach, reading on the beach, lunch, exploring the area, beach, going to the cottage to prepare for supper and then dinner on the same beach. Nature was beautiful, I didn't say that much and Elize was just there. On the one hand I was amazed that she just accepted that I was present the way I was. I thought I wasn't necessarily fun company. Days passed us; it was pleasant. My experiences with my client John had awakened the puzzler in me and although I was not puzzling for myself over how I could feel better, I liked thinking about how better to understand John. I had taken an article with me on how your happiness experience affects whether you are lucky or not. It stated that people who consider themselves lucky, are indeed more fortunate. That hit home, because I really had no luck any more, I was waiting for the next calamity. In the following days I began to fantasize about what happiness actually is. I remembered that when I was twenty or so I found a 25-guilder note in the street.

I couldn't believe it, because I had very little money. Three steps further, I found another 25-guilder note, my surprise changed into fear, because the owner of that money was certain to be around the corner. But nothing could be further from the truth, nobody was there. And sure enough, again a few steps further I found the last 25-guilder note. I felt as happy as a king. After all, I needed the money very badly. That reminder ensured that I got another memory of luck in my head. I decided to write my good-luck memories down one by one. Spontaneously I began to collect pieces of good luck in my head, just as a kind of activity on the beach. In the following days, suddenly something happened in my head, something changed, I felt awake, as if it were getting lighter on the beach...

Once back home, triggered by my experience on the beach, I started spontaneously thinking about a next step. Something I hadn't experienced for a long time, let alone done. In a few weeks my mood changed and I did one discovery after another about my depressive feelings. I started to make models of my experiences and to see if I could transfer what I was experiencing to John as well. Without saying it, I offered John the same ideas (which I had revamped in a coaching format in the meantime) and he had the same experience. I saw him brighten up before my eyes. Step by step I started to investigate what exactly had happened and whether that would apply to other people as well. Some discoveries were immediately clear and with others it took years before I could put into words what I had discovered. Research was to reveal what I and John and my ever-growing group of depressive clients had experienced. In the weeks and months after my first inner change I felt better than ever, awake, and saw how special Elize was. Only then I could (finally) see it. The result of my change is this book. The research that has emerged from my own depressive experience has yielded me a wealth of information and part of it I share by writing *Happiness is Depressing.*

Dejection is a big problem; many people know depressive and dissatisfied feelings. I have come to realize that for us to understand depression better, we must take a hard look at our generally adopted ideas about a happy life. Just like our ideas about what depression is. Our assumptions blur what happiness and depression actually are. I have come to realize that from different assumptions we get different perspectives on how to achieve lasting happiness in our lives. This applies both to the ordinary unsatisfied and to the depressive people among us.

The seven exercises of *ZEST FOR LIFE* aim to make the light shine again in your landscape. Exercise 8 and 9 perpetuate your new landscape. You have worked on zest for life by dismantling the depression gestalt. The light that arises thereby in your landscape is yours. Take initiative and find your way, there are wonderful experiences on your path waiting for you.

Yes, one period in my life I experienced a lot of s... Lucky me!

My inquiry into happiness and depression

In *Happiness is Depressing* I have put happiness and depression under a magnifying glass while going back to the origins of existing definitions and assumptions to explain our dealings with happiness and depression. During my research it became clear that a number of assumptions and definitions about happiness and depression were not applicable to my clients. In addition, I discovered that the current definitions of happiness and depression provide little insight into why my clients felt the way they felt. The definitions and assumptions gave very few handles for a sustainable approach to the feelings of dissatisfaction in my clients. The realization that the assumptions arising from our definition of happiness and depression do not bring us closer to a happy life is the reason for me to question these definitions and assumptions, and with very inspiring and encouraging results.

Method of research

My research does not come from standardized questionnaires in which conclusions are drawn from average outcomes. I speak intensively with people, do interviews and listen to the assumptions, beliefs and descriptions of their experience. I have done this with hundreds of clients and in many groups. I make constant notes of conversations with my clients and listen to the inner structure of a person's experience. Some people have literally drawn their inner landscape for me and others have exactly pointed out what was in front of them, how far away and so on. Over the last ten years I have read a lot of research and delved into it looking for the assumptions our ideas about happiness and depression are based on.

After each interview I search for the corresponding patterns between the experiences of different people. Then I focus entirely on the meaning for the person, because it is precisely that meaning that is relevant. My interpretation of my clients' experience is of minor importance, because it can thwart the understanding of what someone is really experiencing. I look for the hidden problematic assumptions, but also the solutions these assumptions imply. After analysing all the information, a process of testing begins in order to investigate whether I can transfer the knowledge of the research group to other people. I also test myself and everyone around me who is open to it to see if what I have discovered can be transferred to other people. After a lot of testing I come to a model that is transferable to new clients. In this way, step by step, I check every element, of zest for life in this case. This is called *modelling*, which is one of my greatest passions. The goal of modelling is to reveal how the brain (neuro-) works by analysing language patterns (linguistic-) and non-verbal communication. The result of this analysis is worked out into a step-by-step strategy (programming) to transfer to other people.

Classic modelling has investigated successful strategies since the 1970s. This means that instead of the psychological problem being further analysed, its solution is investigated. Positive psychology has only recently turned into a similar path by not only naming the problem but examining how you could become better at something. In this study I have deviated from classical modelling by examining how our current ideas about happiness and depression work. Thus, I have brought to light the problematic ideas behind our current way of thinking about happiness and depression. If you want to know more about this, look under modelling at: www. nlpuniversitypress.com.

Of course, there is much to be learned and discovered. That is why below I describe briefly the most important points of my research. In this way you can see in outline the relevant elements of happiness, depression and zest for life. It is my wish that anyone who has been inspired by the ideas of *Happiness is Depressing* has a springboard to carry forward and expand the research into happiness and depression. This summary may be helpful in this.

If you are interested in my work and method, please visit wassilizafiris.nl. There you will find more information and can contact me if you want to know more about how I work.

HAPPINESS

We refer to two kinds of happiness:
'I'm happy', which denotes the mental-physical state of happiness (being happy).

'I'm lucky', which denotes the experience of having good luck (being fortunate).

1. 'Being happy' is that pleasant state of satisfaction, in which, for no apparent reason or activity, the state of satisfaction (of which it is unclear what we are talking about) is a (spontaneous) part of who we are, our identity.

   → It turns out that people who over-appreciate the state of 'being happy':

   → are more often self-centred, which can lead to feelings of loneliness.

   → are often vague in their objectives, which makes it unclear what they are heading for and makes for disappointment.

   → overvalue feelings of happiness and have a bad relationship with the other emotions, such as sadness, anger, fear and negativity.

   → are very future-oriented, due to which the 'now' is lost sight of.

2. Feeling good in terms of 'being lucky', on the other hand, denotes having 'prosperity', 'favourable circumstances' and even 'being blessed'.

In 'having luck', four subdivisions can be distinguished. These subdivisions turn out to be of great added value to learn how to get out of dejection.

1. Fate - What you have decided - Your destination
2. Prosperity - Advantage - What turns out well - Succeeding - Things work out well
3. Coincidence
4. Light

Depression
The opposite of 'being happy' is 'being unhappy'.
'Being unhappy' describes a feeling of dissatisfaction and often goes hand in hand with depression, nervous strain, anger or sadness.

The opposite of 'good luck, good fortune', is 'bad luck, misfortune'.
'Bad luck' describes an unexpected unpleasant event or condition, adversity, misfortune and even disaster, doom.

Setback & bad luck
When people experience a setback, their fighting spirit and resilience are called upon. When you experience a great deal of adversity, the wretched feeling of misfortune can become so great that all future expectations become negative. You can then develop bad-luck thinking. 'That's me again.' 'Just my luck!' are frequent statements in which the adversity is experienced as a constant experience.
This can cause the world and the people in that world to be perceived as against you or at least as a near calamity. In this situation no or very little influence is experienced on the negative things that we seemingly attract or that happen to us.

Once the world is experienced as an unsafe place, three things happen:

1. Your future perspective changes.
2. You want to 'go inside' instead of 'outward'.
3. Dealing with change becomes increasingly difficult to the point that you can't cope with change any more.

What is depression?
There is no unambiguousness about what depression is. At best, we find descriptions of the *symptoms* of depression in psychiatry. There is also no unambiguousness about the genesis of depression. The lack of clarity in both cases obscures an effective approach.

Current definitions of depression
Depression is, according to current definitions, known as a state of feeling 'dejected', 'down' and 'gloomy'. These definitions became in vogue at the end of the eighteenth century. Contemporary descriptions of course also include words like 'mourning' and 'grief'.

Etymological descriptions of depression
Original descriptions of depression speak of 'oppressing', 'crushing', 'humiliating' and 'weakening' (French meanings from the thirteenth and fourteenth centuries). In the fifteenth century there was talk of 'oppressing' and 'discouraging'. Latin definitions involve concepts such as: 'pressing on', 'injustice' and 'damage'. Related to this are descriptions such as 'humiliate', 'weaken', 'be afraid', 'reject' and 'reduce in value'.

Interesting and at the same time crucial in understanding depression are the differences in modern and original definitions.

The modern descriptions of depression refer to personal states of mind. For example, 'dejected' describes the state of the person who is dejected. Virtually all original definitions of depression describe actions from the outside. Take for example: 'press down', 'crush', 'humiliate', 'weaken', 'discourage', and 'reject'. These are all descriptions of an external force which seeks to suppress a person's spirit, an act of a person or group aimed at another person or group. These descriptions come close to the inner experience that clients describe when they speak about their dejection.

A problem without a solution
There is no description of a solution for depression. When you are depressed it is unclear what you should be striving for. The goal is unknown. No 'opposite' of depression has been described so far.

The causes of depression
There is no unambiguousness about what exactly causes depression. DSM-thinking mainly involves a physiological (substance) explanation. While there is certainly evidence that hormones and neurotransmitters play a role, it is too simple to say that these substances are the cause of depression. People are meaning-creating beings and our interpretation of an experience influences our state of mind. Any other state of mind is influenced and possibly even created by other areas in our brain and other chemicals. However, it is meaning that activates these substances. Human beings are therefore also products of their circumstances and the significance attributed to these circumstances. We can therefore point out three causes of depression, which I have found in my research: 1. Loneliness 2. A suddenly changing self-image. 3. Chronic setback. If you are dealing with two of these causes, chances are that the depressive gestalt may arise.

The influence of DSM thinking
'DSM thinking' has influenced us in how we think about depression.
In the Handbook for Psychiatric Disorders, depression is a disease and that is not strange because the DSM is written by doctors. Doctors view processes logically in terms of illness and health and a disease can be treated from a medical point of view by intervening surgically or medicinally.
In addition, the DSM only describes the problem and not the solution.

The symptoms are generalized and very aspecific, so the internal perception and experience of a depressed person are unclear.

Symptom Complex
Depression is also not easy to grasp, but you could say that most forms of low spirits, dejection and depressive episodes are not a disease but a symptom complex, created by a fairly precisely brought together amalgam of thoughts and feelings about yourself, others and the world, about the past and the future. From this frames of mind have emerged from which conclusions have been drawn and decisions taken until the depressive gestalt is a reality.

External forces
In depression, clients experience external forces that are larger than they can handle. 'The world' and all the uncontrollable setbacks that the world can inflict on you are such external forces. These external forces are making the world 'beyond' an increasingly unsafe place where disaster, great misfortune, threat, grim prospects, misery, danger, evil, fate, trouble, sinister affairs and difficulties lie ahead.

Inner landscape
A depressed person (like everyone else) has an inner experience, which I call the 'inner landscape'. The thing is that we are generally unaware of this landscape. However, it constitutes an invisible filter through which we perceive the world around us. The inner landscape of a depressed person is characterized by darkness, among other things. It is literally dark in the inside world of the person and this creates as it were a room, a room in which the person is shut off from the world outside it. The person in question may not be aware of this inner dark empty space. A world that is unsafe and even turned against us means that we increasingly withdraw mentally and emotionally. Eventually, we have withdrawn so far that we end up in a 'dark room', an inside world where there is no emotional awareness of 'outside' anymore. Shut off from the world

around us. In this room you are also alone. Lonely feelings are created by people and a world that rejects them. This is a trigger for the coming into being of the enclosed space. And in a dark room where you have no idea of where the exit is, the only thing left is waiting for a possible liberation.

Every effort to work effectively with dejection begins where you are, in that darkroom. That means that there is a need for courage and trust to learn to experience what is really going on with you.

Gestalt

A gestalt is a phenomenon that you can no longer resolve into the independent parts it was constructed from. Depression is a gestalt state of mind. To transform a gestalt, it is important to investigate which are the key elements that are decisive in the development of the gestalt. The depression gestalt consists of an aggregate of building blocks that, combined in a unique manner, cause depression. Offering a solution aimed at only part of the molecule cannot change the whole, unless you are lucky...

Unachievable goals

Depressive people often pursue great nonspecific goals such as: (wanting) to be happy. The grandeur and unspecifiedness of this endeavour causes two important things: First, because of the vagueness of the objective, it is nearly impossible to achieve it. What is more important, though, is that neither good luck nor happiness exist in the darkness of the depressive person, it is a pursuit outside the dark room of which one does not know where the exit is. Taking this state of affairs into account ensures that grand, nonspecific and unachievable goals are absurd goals. Absurd because the future perception of a depressed person has disappeared and the world outside the room does not exist. In this manner, just by wishing 'I simply want to be happy' the infeasibility of this wish is directly translated into a deepening of the dejection.

Creating awareness

The solution to this problem begins by generating the awareness that the person in question is in a dark room, so that from there the effective definition of happiness can really be made, which is 'creating the felt experience of prosperity'. This yields light and an opening in the dark room, so that a first sense of direction can be awakened. Then, depending on which of the three elements prevail, we can work towards more bonding and a healthy self-image.

ZEST FOR LIFE

The opposite of depressed is 'zest for life'. The desire to live and to keep on living. Only when we know what we are looking for can we try to find it. And only when we know that we need the experience of 'having good luck' (prosperity), 'zest for life' to go for, and that we can only start from the perspective of where we are, the door can come ajar to another experience.

Being lucky

So, in order to find a bright spot in the darkness, it is important to realize where you are. As we said, we are pursuing a wrong brand of happiness. Instead of going for 'being happy' you want to get the experience of prosperity, 'being lucky' back on your retina. Why? The feeling of prosperity activates the expectation that things will be going well, might go well. The feeling of prosperity creates a future awareness, a 'way out', an active experience in which the sense of 'I can do something about this' can wake up again.

Solving depression

To solve depression once and for all, it is important not to work only on part of the depressive state of mind but on the whole. You want to deconstruct the depressive gestalt by activating the elements of zest for life. But it also requires a changing awareness of what happiness is for us, so that you can pursue the right form of happiness, namely 'having luck'. To transform loneliness, it is important to

activate connection and bonding, to update your changed
self-image by healing and restoring the connection with
yourself. It is important to stir up the feeling of influence
so that you can take the right actions at the right time.
In the case of dejection, the right place is the depressive
landscape itself and nothing outside it. The sense of
influence helps you to change your interpretation style.
Only then can you work on the most essential feeling of
happiness that we need, the feeling of 'being lucky'. The
new inner landscape that this combination of elements
causes to appear, is one where the light can shine again
and zest for life can begin.

'Slowly, I emerged from the
darkness, gingerly, quietly,
but I felt it happening... and
it was quite extraordinary.'

Giles Andreae

Afterword

Thank you for having taken the time to read *Happiness is Depressing* and to experience how you can feel high-spirited again. You have become acquainted with all kinds of processes to get more awareness about yourself and a method to achieve profound change.

This book could not have been created in this form if I had not been supported by crucial people. It has been of great value to me that people have read along with me. The renewed view of my work after each feedback round has stimulated my development tremendously. While writing this book I have learned to really let go. There are parts of the book I had been working on for months, which I have yet rewritten prompted by the keen feedback of my readers. Sometimes this was painful but after each feedback round the book became better. I would like to thank Tessa Jol because she kept reading along and kept coming up with suggestions, even though she was very busy. Tessa commands a view of the whole and makes apt remarks completely *out of the box*. I would like to thank Aranka van der Pol for being a tower of strength, leaving her door always open and continuing to think along with me, even when it is in the middle of the night. I would like to thank Nienke van Oeveren for the completely fresh look she has given my book. Thank you so much!

Translating *Happiness is Depressing* in English after the initial publishing in Dutch in 2016 has been a very rewarding experience. I want to especially thank Lucas Derks for promoting my work and his continuous support and positive feedback. I also want to thank Tim Hallbom for his time and interest in my work. Both men are, in their own rights, icons in the field of NLP and lovely human beings. I also want to thank Hein de Jong, a renowned Dutch psychiatrist, for his immediate trust and support of my work. Thank you, Hein. I especially want to thank Gert Arts, a long-time colleague of mine and translator of *Happiness is Depressing*. Thank you, Gert, for all the effort you have put into a great translation! Many others come to mind not in the least my clients. Due to my research many more depressed clients knocked on my door than I could anticipate. I want to thank you for your trust and your vulnerability.

The processes you have been able to read and practice have been developed and tested by me. I can imagine that you would like to learn how to apply these exercises even better to yourself or to use them with others. In addition to the range of trainings and opportunities for personal coaching that you can find on my site (www.wassilizafiris. nl), I have developed training courses, specifically on the themes of this book. For example, I offer a three-day training session for depressive or dissatisfied people to learn the themes that have emerged in this book in depth. The *Depression and zest for life* training can be a life-changing experience for you. In addition to the trainings aimed at personal change and development, I also offer a training for professionals, specifically for coaches, therapists, psychotherapistst and hypnotherapists who want to learn great new coaching methods for working with depressive people. This is a unique training, if only because a coaching training for this theme does not exist yet. The training *Depression and zest-for-life coach* is an intensive and very inspiring training in which you learn the best coaching techniques and their backgrounds to work fully focused with this complex matter. If you want to know more about the training courses or possibilities for personal assistance, please contact me via the site. I wish you a lot of light and zest for life!
Wassili Zafiris

Reference list

American Psychiatric Association, *Diagnostic and Statistical Manual of Mental Disorders*, fourth edition, DSM-IV, Washington DC, 2005.

American Psychiatric Association, *Diagnostic and Statistical Manual of Mental Disorders*, fifth edition, DSM-V, Washington DC, 2018.

Andreae, Giles, *Purple Ronnie creator on depression: I lost the gift of joy for a while*, The Timesonline, 23 november 2009.

Andreas, Steve, *Becoming Lucky*, realpeoplepress.com, 2008.

Andreas, Steve, *Transforming Your Self: Becoming Who You Want to Be*, 2002.

Baumeister, Roy F., *Wilskracht (Willpower)*, Nieuwezijds, 2011.

Bhattacharyya, Anindya, *The politics of depression: Mark Fisher on mental health and class confidence*, rs21, www.rs21.org.uk, 27 april, 2014.

Bolstad, R. & Hamblett, M., *NLP And The Rediscovery Of Happiness*, www.transformations.net.nz.

Bolstad, R. & Hamblett, M., *Transforming Communication*, Longman, Auckland, 1998.

Boseley, Sarah, *Two-thirds of Britons with depression get no treatment*, The Guardian, 13 augustus 2014.

Briggs, Helen, *Depression: 'second biggest cause of disability' in the world*, BBC News, 6 november 2013.

Brooks, Arthur C. Dr., *Gross National Happiness*, Basic Books, april 2008.

Bruder, Jessica, *The Psychological Price of Entrepreneurship*, Inc. Magazine, september 2013.

Burkeman, Oliver, *Happiness is a glass half empty*, The Guardian, 15 juni 2012.

Burkeman, Oliver, *The Antidote: Happiness for People Who Can't Stand Positive Thinking*, Canongate Books; Main edition, 3.

CBS (Centraal Bureau for Statistics, Dutch Central Agency of Statistics): *More than 1 million Dutch had depression*, 25 January 2016.

Curtis, Adam, *The Trap: What Happened to Our Dream of Freedom*, BBC2, 2007.

Davidson, Richard, Dr., *The Emotional Life of Your Brain: How Its Unique Patterns Affect the Way You Think, Feel, and Live--and How You Can Change Them*, Plume, 2012.

Derks, Lucas, *Social Panoramas: Changing the Unconscious Landscape, with NLP and Psychotherapy*, Crown House Publishing 2005.

Dickson, Joanne Dr., *People with depression tend to pursue generalised goals*, University of Liverpool, Institute of Psychology -University News, 8 juli 2013.

Fenwick Elliott Annabel, *A nation of solo eaters: How the death of the traditional family household means we eat over half of our meals alone - Research from the Family Dinner Project*, Daily Mail online, 8 augustus 2014.

Viktor Frankl, *Man's Search for Meaning: An introduction to Logo therapy*, 1945-1978.

Gruber, June, *Four Ways Happiness Can Hurt You*, Greater Good, mei 2011.

Hall, L. Michael, Ph.D., *Emotional tolerance for accepting all emotion*, www.neurosemantics.com, juli 2013.

Hall, L. Michael, Ph.D., Rose-Charvet, Shelle (red.), *Innovations in NLP for Challenging Times*, 2011, Crown House Publising, 2011. Hoofdstuk: Roberts, Martin, *The Well Formed Problem*.

Hall, L. Michael, Ph.D, *Meta-States: Mastering the Higher States of Your Mind*, V.S., Neuro-Semantic Publications, 2000.

Hall, L. Michael, Ph.D., *Neuro-Semantics: Actualizing Meaning and Performance*, Neuro-Semantic Publications, 2011.

Hall, L. Michael, Ph.D., *Nlp Going Meta: Advanced Modeling Using Meta-Levels*, Neuro-Semantic Publications, 1997.

Hall, L. Michael, Ph.D., *The Matrix Model, The 7 Matrices of Neuro-Semantics*, V.S., Neuro-Semantic Publications, 2003.

Hari, Johann, *The Likely Cause of Addiction Has Been Discovered, and It Is Not What You Think*, Huffington Post, 20 januari 2015.

Harris, Thomas, *I am Ok, You're Ok*, Harper & Row, 1967.

Hayes, Steven C., Strosahl, Kirk D., *Acceptance and Commitment Therapy: The Process and Practice of Mindful Change*, The Guilford Press, 2011.

Jeffries, Stuart, about Jacques Peretti's TV series The Men Who Made Us Spend BBC2: *SUVs, handwash and FOMO: how the advertising industry embraced fear*, The Guardian, 7 juli 2014.

Klein, Stefan, *The Happinnesformula: how good feelings arise*, Ambo, 2003.

Köhler, Wim, nrc.checkt, woensdag 28 januari 2016.

Kringelbach, Morten L., Berridge Kent C., *The Neuroscience of Happiness and Pleasure*, PMC, US National Library of Medicine, juli 2011.

Lombardo, Elizabeth, *Better Than Perfect*, Seal Press, 2014.

Lyubomirsky, Sonja, *The how of happiness*, Penguin Books, 2008.

Mandela, Nelson, *Long Walk to Freedom: The Autobiography of Nelson Mandela*, Abacus, 1995.

Mantel, Arianne, *Alarm om toename zelfdodingen* (*Alarm about increase suicides*) Telegraaf 22 mei 2014.

Mauss, Iris B., Tamir, Maya, Anderson, Craig L., Savino, Nicole S., *Can Seeking Happiness Make People Happy? Paradoxical Effects of Valuing Happiness*, Emotion, augustus 2011.

Oettingen, Gabriele, *Rethinking Positive Thinking*, Current, 2014.

Oxford Dictionary of English Etymology, and several online dictionaries.

Peters, Frances, van Dijk, Arjan, *Hoe haal je de sekte uit het voormalig sektelid?* (*How do you get the sect out of the former sect member?*) Uit: Special'Dag van de coach'van het tijdschrift voor coaching, (from: Special 'Day of the Coach' of the *Magazine for coaching*) juni 2015.

Raison, Charles Dr., *Should grief be treated like depression?*, Special to CNN, 17 februari 2012.

Redactie Wetenschap, *Psychotherapie helpt maar matig tegen depressie*, Trouw, 2 maart 2010, (Science Desk, *Psychotherapy only moderately works against depression*, Trouw) 2 March 2010.

Rosenberg, Marshall, *Nonviolent Communication: A language of Life*, Puddledanser Press, 2003.

Seligman, Martin E. P., *Flourish: A Visionary New Understanding of Happiness and Well-being*, VS, Atria Books, 2012.

Seligman, Martin E. P., *Authentic Happiness: Using the New Positive Psychology to Realize Your Potential for Lasting Fulfillment*, VS, Atria Books, 2004.

Sharot, Tali, *The Optimism Bias*, The Guardian, 1 januari 2012.

Sifferlin, Alexandra, *This is the Equation for Happiness*, Times.com, 4 augustus 2014.

Tierney, John, *A New Gauge to See What's Beyond Happiness*, The New York Times 16 mei 2011.

Topping, Alexandra, *One in 10 do not have a close friend and even more feel unloved, survey finds*, The Guardian, 12 augustus 2014.

Tylor, Edward Burnett, *Researches into the Early History of Mankind and the Development of Civilization*, V.K., Estes & Lauriat, 1865.

Wedge, Marilyn, *Why French kids don't have ADHD*, Psychology Today, maart 2012.

Wind, Chris, *Jong, somber en verdrietig: depressie tijdens studie* (*Young, sombre and sad: depression during college*), Hanzemag.nl, 26 februari 2015.

Wiseman, Richard, *The Luck Factor; Changing Your Luck, Changing Your Life*, Miramax, 2003.

Yapko, M.D., *Hypnosis And The Treatment Of Depressions*, Brunner/Mazel, 1992.

Zafiris, Wassili, *Geluk is deprimerend: de coachopleiding voor coaches, hulpverleners en psychologen om werkelijk geluk te faciliteren*, handleiding (*Depression and Zest for Life Coaching Training*, Training Manual), 2010.

Zafiris, Wassili, *Weerbaarheid & Veerkracht*, handleiding, 2004-2016. (*Resilience Training*, Training Manual, 2004-2019).

Zafiris, Wassili , Steenstra, Ben, *IK BEN niet alleen op de wereld*, Academic Service, 2011 (to be published in English as *Meaningful Profit*).

Zuidhof, Marie-Anne, *De duivelse DSM-V, (the devilish DSM-V)*, De kennis van nu (*Today's knowledge*) De kennis van nu, NPO, 24 mei 2013.

Other references

Antibacterial soap with triclosan'no better at killing germs'– study, The Guardian, 16 september 2015.

Depressiesymptomen DSM-V: kenmerken en behandeling, (*Syptoms of Depression DSM-V: Characteristics and treatment*), Mens en Samenleving: Psychologie, november 2011.

Het Supermansyndroom (*The Superman syndrome*) blog on www.wassilizafiris.nl, 1 september 2013.

Helpless to optimism, video on www.wassilizafiris.nl, 7 oktober 2013.

Interview Antonie Kamerling, *Het Hoogste Woord* (*Hogging the Limelight*), Klaas Drupsteen, NCRV, 26 december 2007.

Mensen zijn net konijnen (*People are just like rabbits*), blog verschenen op www.wassilizafiris.nl, 14 april 2014.

Metaphores of Movement, Andrew Austin, www.metaphorsofmovement.co.uk.

Neurosemantiek, www.neurosemantics.com.

Ondernemen op eenzame hoogte (*Doing business on lonely heights*) blog on www.wassilizafiris.nl, 12 oktober 2015.

Transformers, director Michael Bay, Universal Pictures, 2007.

For a complete depression questionnaire see *Depressie en levenslustcoachopleiding,* (*Depression and zest for life-coach training*) www.wassilizafiris.nl.

Websites consulted

www.brainyquote.com/quotes/keywords/rejection.html
www.etymonline.com
www.freedictionairy.com
www.gripopjedip.nl
www.nl.wikipedia.org
www.who.int/mental_health
www.wiktionary.org

"For more than 4 years I had sunk really low, I had tried virtually all therapies and pills. I was caught in a vicious circle with thoughts no one understood, I thought.
Until I met Wassili. He considered my doom-thoughts as metaphors. With his enormous, scientifically based knowledge as well as his vast experience, he knows why you think what you think. Finally, someone who truly understood me and who had solutions to 'change my inner landscape'. It changed my life. This man is a wizard with words."

Gerben Kessen, Entrepreneur

Biography

Wassili Zafiris (1964) is NLP master trainer, coach, researcher, author, public speaker. He has 25 years of experience in the fields of personal and organisational change. He was the mental coach of the Dutch Women's Volleyball team.

In 2017 he received a fellowship from the International Institute of Organisational Psychological Medicine. *Stress and relaxation in the workplace,* for the *Oxford Textbook of Organisational Psychological Medicine,* will be published in the course of 2020.

In *Happiness is Depressing* (2019, first published in Dutch in 2016) he describes his ground-breaking coaching method of transforming depression into Zest for life. *Happiness is Depressing* is a step by step guide (for professionals *and* clients) to transform the main causes of depression: loneliness, adversity, negative self-image. Wassili is co-author of the twice nominated book *Meaningful Profit** (Best Business book 2011, Best Management book 2012) about his applied research of personal leadership and resilience during organisational transformation. In 2008 he co-authored *Appetite*** about the mindset of the best chef cooks in the world.

He is co-developer of the business model *Meaningful Profit* and Faculty member of the Global School for Entrepreneurship and Innovation. He teaches Masterclasses 'Leadership' at Nyenrode Business University. Wassili developed the model *Driven by Nature* about the essential drives of people. He is past board member of the Dutch ICF (International Coach Federation) and fulfilled European posts for the ICF. He has a passion for nature and is Climate Leader with Al Gore.

In Dutch: **IK BEN niet alleen op de wereld **EETlust*

Wassili Zafiris can be contacted through his website: www.wassilizafiris.nl/en

9 789090 320427